Buttermilk Cookbook:

The Rest of the Carton

Susan Costello & Anna Heller

Bonus Books, Inc., Chicago

00 99 98 97 96   5 4 3 2 1

Library of Congress Cataloging-in-Publication Data

Costello, Susan.
     Buttermilk cookbook: the rest of the carton / Susan, Costello &
Anna Heller. —1st ed.
         p. cm.
     Includes index
     ISBN 1–56625–060–9
     1. Cookery (Sour cream and milk) 2. Buttermilk. I. Heller,
Anna. II. Title.
     TX759.5.S68C67 1996
     641.6'724—dc20   96–13296

Bonus Books, Inc.
160 East Illinois Street
Chicago, Illinois 60611

Cover, book design and illustrations
by John E. Merrill

First Edition

Printed in the United States of America

TABLE OF CONTENTS

ACKNOWLEDGEMENTS

Our thanks to:

- Our mothers, who raised us to believe we could do anything.

- Anna's husband, Bill, and son, Bubba, who were supportive and well-behaved.

- Susan's dear friend, John Merrill, who painstakingly prepared our manuscript and did the charming illustrations.

- Our neighbors and co-workers, who never tired of taste-testing.

- Bonus Books for their encouragement and support.

FOREWORD

Cooking for many of us is a way to demonstrate our special creativity and love for others who bring meaning to our lives. Around the globe, cooks have treasured recipes using buttermilk as the prized ingredient for mouth-watering and unique concoctions. The recipes in *Buttermilk Cookbook: The Rest of the Carton* will show your family and friends just how creative you are as a cook. The best part is that you will be serving dishes that use buttermilk, a product that is naturally low in fats and calories and rich in protein, vitamins and minerals.

Buttermilk and other dairy products are known as nearly perfect foods because of the rich array of nutrients they contain. Today, nutritionists and health professionals are encouraging all segments of our population to consume more nutrient-dense foods such as buttermilk on a daily basis.

The good news is that buttermilk is made from low-fat or skim milk and contains about 90 calories per eight-ounce serving! More than 100 nutritional components have been discovered in buttermilk. Buttermilk is an excellent source of high-quality protein; nearly 40 percent of buttermilk solids contain protein. Protein builds and repairs tissue, helps form antibodies, and furnishes energy.

Vitamins A, D, E and K, all found in buttermilk, aid the body in maintaining skin and mucosal tissue, depositing calcium properly onto the skeleton, ensuring the proper use of vitamin A, and help the process of blood clotting. Buttermilk is an important source of riboflavin, or vitamin B-2, which is involved in the oxidation of glucose and fatty acids.

The major mineral needed by the human body, calcium, is found in high concentration in buttermilk. Calcium builds and strengthens bones and teeth, helps muscles to contract and relax, aids in blood clotting and protects against high blood pressure.

Traditionally, buttermilk was the liquid remaining after cream was made into butter. Today, buttermilk does not come in contact with butter during the entire fermentation process. Buttermilk is cultured from pasteurized or ultra-pasteurized lowfat or skim milk to produce consistent results. Buttermilk gets its buttery taste from streptococcus lactis, which is added to develop the acid and produces buttermilk's aroma. Milk is incubated at temperatures between 68° Fahrenheit and 72° Fahrenheit for approximately 12 to 14 hours or until the desired acidity of 0.8 to 0.9 percent lactic acid occurs. The fermentation process is stopped by stirring and cooling. The manufacturer may add liquid butter or butter flakes to buttermilk to give the product the straight-from-the-churn appearance. Salt, citric acid or sodium citrate may be added to improve the flavor.

I hope you will enjoy showing off your creative cooking flair by using such a healthy product as buttermilk.

To good eating and to good health!

Grace Hilt-Mack, M.S., C.F.C.S.
Nutritionist and
Former Regional Coordinator for the Dairy Council, Inc.

INTRODUCTION

Most cooks have a few favorite recipes that call for buttermilk. Frequently, these recipes are handed down from generation to generation and evoke fond memories and feelings of well-being. Mother's chocolate cake and grandma's cornbread have become family traditions that mark special occasions or celebrate the advent of certain seasons.

Other cooks may have learned about the essence of buttermilk from a favorite celebrity chef, a sophisticated food magazine or from chatting with other food lovers in cyberspace.

Whatever the case, one question is common to all: *What to do with the reset of the carton*? The idea for this book came when we found ourselves pouring the unused portion of the carton down the drain. We originally set out to simply answer that question. But, like in all of life's pursuits, we met up with some wonderful, unexpected surprises along the way.

Many of the recipes we visited — BISCUITS, DUMPLINGS, SHORTCAKES & COBBLERS and PANCAKES, WAFFLES & FRENCH TOAST — were familiar uses for buttermilk. It was a joy to explore the unique goodness imparted by this low-fat ingredient.

As we moved on to other areas — CAKES & FROSTINGS; QUICK BREADS & COFFEE CAKES; MUFFINS & DOUGHNUTS; SCONES; COOKIES & CONFECTIONS; CHEESECAKES, PIES & FROZEN DELIGHTS; YEAST BREADS and PIZZAS — we delighted in discovering how well buttermilk enhances the flavor and texture of foods typically made with other types of dairy products.

Some of our best cooking adventures were in the realms of APPETIZERS, BEVERAGES, SNACKS & SPREADS; MAIN DISHES and SOUPS, SALADS & SIDE DISHES — where we marveled at how well buttermilk complements other good ingredients.

We had a wonderful time creating and testing these 250 recipes. At the end of the book is a unique appended index, which lists these recipes by the quantity of buttermilk used to make sure you get maximum use of your buttermilk. By the time you get to this index, you'll no longer wonder what to do with the rest of the carton.

Happy cooking!

BUTTERMILK FACTS

WHAT'S IN THAT CARTON ANYWAY?

Despite its name, there's virtually no butterfat in buttermilk. An eight-ounce cup of buttermilk made from one-percent milk contains only 2.5 grams of fat, which is just four percent of the average daily allotment.

Buttermilk was originally a by-product of making — surprise — butter! Cream was collected from a few milkings (and since it usually took several days to amass enough cream, it was slightly soured by airborne bacteria) and churned until the fat globules massed together. The liquid remaining after the butter was removed was basically "skimmed" milk that was slightly soured.

When everyone kept a few cows and made butter for home use or sale, buttermilk was a common household substance. And, since frugality was a virtue, it was widely used as a beverage and baking ingredient.

Now that few of us have our own cows and even fewer of us churn our own butter, we can only get buttermilk that is prepared commercially. Batches of churn leavings from butter are no longer sufficiently or uniformly soured to produce a consistent buttermilk product. As they do with sour cream, commercial dairies take skim or low-fat milk and inoculate it with a bacterial culture that thickens it and imparts a tangy flavor. The cultured product behaves essentially like the original in baking and in other culinary processes.

HOW TO BUY BUTTERMILK

Although buttermilk has a longer shelf life than uncultured milks, there are different degrees of freshness. We prefer to use buttermilk for beverages when it's as young — and thin — as possible. There are two useful tests. First, choose a carton with the most distant pull date. Remember, however, that poor handling techniques after the carton leaves the dairy can prematurely age the contents. So, secondly, shake the cartons and listen for the most fluid-sounding one. Thicker, but still fresh, buttermilk is perfectly fine for non-beverage recipes.

Buttermilk cultures remain active even after the processors fill the cartons. If you've ever let an open carton of buttermilk "ripen" in your refrigerator, you may have noticed that it became thicker and "clumpier" after a few days. This continued ripening does not really affect buttermilk's effectiveness in cooking or baking. If, however, the buttermilk has separated into a clear liquid and thick chunks, it's spoiled.

HOME-BREWED BUTTERMILK

Batches of buttermilk can be cultured at home. Save 1/2 cup of butter-milk to use as a "starter." Add the buttermilk to 1 quart of fresh skim milk. Shake well and refrigerate for a couple of days. The process can be accel-erated by letting the mixture sit at room temperature for several hours before refrigerating.

HOMEMADE CHEESE

In a large stock pot, combine 4 cups buttermilk and 1 gallon of regular milk (any fat content you prefer). Over medium-low heat, bring the mix-ture to 95°. Meanwhile, cut a rennet tablet in quarters. (If you can't find rennet tablets, use 1/4 cup lemon juice or cider vinegar.) Crush 1/4 tablet and stir in 1/4 cup water. Stir rennet mixture into warmed milk. Turn off heat and let pot sit on burner 10 minutes until mixture thickens. Do not stir or remove from pot. With a long knife, cut the thickened mixture into 1" squares by drawing the knife into the cheese in a tic-tac-toe design to form curds. Turn the heat back on to medium-low and heat the curds to 115°, without stirring. Line a colander with 2 layers of cheesecloth. Gently stir 1 teaspoon salt and any desired seasoning into the curds. Turn out into colan-der and let drain. Discard the drained whey. Keep the cheese in the colander. Cover top with cheesecloth. Place a plate on top of the cheese and top with a heavy weight like a large can or a rock. Continue to drain about 1 hour. Chill and serve. Keep cheese refrigerated.

BUTTERMILK FUN AND FORMULAS

BUTTER from CREAM — BUTTERMILK from BUTTER

Here's a silly exercise that shows how buttermilk was originally made.

Mix together too much time on your hands and the advice of a wacky friend like Anna. Set aside.

Beat a perfectly good pint of heavy cream or crème fraîche way past the whipped stage. After what seems like forever, the mixture will become almost granular and then fat globules will suddenly coagulate into chunks of butter that will stick to the beater(s). Remove the butter. The liquid left is (not much) buttermilk! Rinse the butter solids in cold water, add salt and enjoy.

BUTTERMILK ART

If finger-paints aren't messy enough...

Paint a thin coat of buttermilk over the drawing paper. While still wet, draw a picture with chalk directly onto the surface. Let dry.

a paint brush
buttermilk
white drawing paper
colored chalk(s)

BUTTERMILK BEAUTY

From a 19th-century "infomercial":

Buttermilk is an acid product like sour cream or yogurt. This is probably why it was promoted as a facial for erasing freckles. We're not sure it works, but it can't hurt.

SEPTIC TANK FORMULA

Septic tank solids are slowly digested by bacteria. This formula purports to encourage bacterial growth. We have municipal sewers, so we offer no guarantees.

Mix together and pour down the drain. Use monthly.

2 packets active dry yeast
1/2 cup brown sugar
1/2 quart buttermilk
1 gallon warm water

MAKING MOSS

Joan from Jersey swears by this.

Use a mixture of half buttermilk and half water to encourage the growth of moss on tree-shaded areas of your lawn.

WORDS of WISDOM and UNABASHED OPINIONS

After 15 years of friendship and 50 years of combined cooking experience, we thought we knew all about each other and cooking when we started testing the recipes for this book. Sixty quarts of buttermilk later, we're amazed at what we learned about food and friendship. The friendship lesson is simple — You may always be right, but let your friend be "righter."

The cooking instructions are a little more complicated. What follows here and at the beginning of several of the following chapters are proven tips and stubborn opinions.

Ingredients: The best ingredients yield the best results

Baking Powder — Exposure to air or moisture can enervate baking powder. It's important to test baking powder for effervescence if you don't use it frequently. Drop a little in water, put it up to your ear and listen for fizzing. Write the date of purchase on the next can you buy and start testing it before using after about six months. A few brands of baking powder are available without aluminum compounds. We think these are healthier and taste better.

Baking Soda — An even more historic chemical leavening agent than baking powder, soda works best in an acid environment, such as the one created by buttermilk. Baking soda also has a limited shelf life and is vulnerable to air or moisture exposure. Test its potency by mixing it with a little vinegar. You should get a tiny volcano of bubbles. Write the date of purchase on the next box you buy.

Brown Sugar — We prefer dark brown sugar for most purposes. It has a stronger flavor and richer color. Brown sugar is always packed tightly when measured.

Butter — We prefer its flavor and cooking qualities over other fats for most purposes. Although there were a few occasions when we used other fats to meet textural or traditional taste requirements, we generally used butter. Don't, however, use butter in frying or other activities requiring high temperatures since it burns easily. Butter has a respectable shelf life in the refrigerator and freezes well, if necessary.

Cheeses — Different cheeses have very distinctive flavors. In this book, we primarily used cheddar (we prefer extra sharp), parmesan, romano (please don't use pre-ground canister cheese) and feta. Imported parmesan, romano and feta cheeses are, unfortunately, more flavorful than domestic cheeses. Use what you like best, but do try some new varieties. If you grate and shred cheeses yourself, you'll get pieces the size you desire; you'll also be able to use a greater variety and higher quality, and you'll save money.

Chocolate for Baking — There are five basic types of bakers or baking chocolate: unsweetened, bitter, semi-sweet, sweet and milk chocolate. Their characteristics are quite different, so you will get the best results if you use what the recipe calls for. Buy the best quality you can afford. Never substitute chocolate morsels for baking chocolate.

Citrus Fruits — The use of freshly squeezed lemon, lime and orange juice, as well as freshly grated citrus zest (peels), will make or break a recipe when they're called for. One lemon or lime yields about three tablespoons of juice and a scant tablespoon of zest. For future convenience, grate the zest from all your citrus fruits before you eat them and store them airtight in your freezer. They are a wonderful flavor enhancer and well worth the effort. Some produce handlers wax citrus fruit. Rinse them in hot water if you're not sure if they've been treated.

Cocoa — Many of the recipes in this book require unsweetened powdered baking cocoa. Don't use the sweetened mixes intended for beverages.

Cornmeal — Stone-ground cornmeal has the best texture both as an ingredient and for dusting baking sheets to keep doughs from sticking. It does go rancid, so buy it in amounts you can use within two or three months. Store it airtight to keep those weevils away.

Dried Fruits — Cooks of yesteryear relied on raisins, currants, figs and dates to add sweetness to their baked goods. Improved drying processes now bring a greater variety to the grocer's shelf, including cranberries, cherries, blueberries, mangos, pineapple, and papaya, among others. Stored airtight, they have an almost limitless shelf life and can be substituted for each other in just about any recipe.

Eggs — Our recipes were prepared with large eggs. The color doesn't matter.

Flours — All-purpose flour is probably the most common flour in American kitchens and, as its name implies, can be used for most purposes. If you can manage it, you should also stock some of the specialized wheat flours we have called for, such as bread, cake, whole wheat, and semolina. They contribute significantly to the desired results. We have also used flours milled from other grains and plants such as rye and buckwheat. Don't expect quite the same results if you substitute all-purpose flour for those specified. Flours do have a shelf life. White wheat flours will last for several months. Whole grain flours will last not quite so long. A quick taste will let you know if they've gone rancid. Buy flours you plan to use less often in small quantities from health food stores or other markets offering bulk sales. Most flours today do not require sifting before measuring. Sifting, however, is a great way to assure that the flour mixes well with the other dry ingredients in a recipe. You'll find more information on the uses of various flours in the body of this book.

Garlic — Always use fresh garlic or garlic that has been roasted and frozen. For easy peeling, snip off tiny bits at both ends, lay the garlic clove on a flat surface and squash it slightly with a flat surface or the side of a broad knife. The peel will come right off.

Herbs — Both fresh and dried herbs have their uses. Fresh herbs are generally brighter, but not always available. As a general rule, use one teaspoon dried herbs for one tablespoon chopped fresh herbs. Basil and parsley are best fresh. When dried, they taste like lawn clippings.

Maple Syrup — Real syrup from the tree is indescribably better. Read the label carefully.

Mayonnaise — We used only "real" mayonnaise with the blue ribbon on the label.

Molasses — Our taste preference is for unsulphured molasses.

Nutmeg — Freshly grated really does taste better. Nutmeg graters are available for a dollar or less.

Nuts — Toasted nuts have a richer flavor. Most nuts can be toasted on a dry baking sheet in a 350° oven in about 10 minutes. Be careful not to burn them. Nuts have a lot of oil and can go rancid, even in unopened packages. Store nuts in airtight containers in the refrigerator or freezer. Taste for freshness before using.

Olive Oil — We specified olive oil in several recipes where its flavor is vital to the taste and texture of the creation. We think you will be disappointed if you substitute a neutral vegetable oil. Buy olive oil in quantities you will use within a month or two. Oil, olive or otherwise, with rancid overtones will ruin a dish. We used extra-virgin olive oil for most purposes because we like its fruity flavor best.

Pepper — Freshly ground pepper has a more sparkling taste.

Salt — We prefer coarse kosher salt because it is free of odd-tasting chemicals.

Spices — Buy these relatively expensive flavoring agents in small amounts you can use within six or eight months. Ethnic grocery stores or health food stores generally offer significantly cheaper as well as fresher, better-quality spices. We have been known to grind and sift whole spices for better flavor but we don't insist you do it. Keep spices in airtight containers.

Vanilla Extract — Use only pure vanilla extract. The other stuff makes things taste BAD.

Tools: Making life easier

Baking Pans and Sheets — Always try to use the pan sizes specified by a recipe. If you must substitute, try to use a pan of about equal volume (fill pans with measuring cups of water to compare them) and adjust temperatures or times to compensate, testing more frequently for doneness.

Baking Papers — Parchment paper is extremely useful, particularly in assuring that layer cakes turn out of the pan without breaking. For years, we took our chances with just greasing and flouring cake pans. A few dessert disasters convinced us to line greased pans with parchment circles. Parchment is also a good liner for baking sheets. You can use wax paper to line cake pans but not baking sheets, because the high temperatures make the wax coating smoke and melt and make a real mess. Aluminum muffin cup liners are a real time-saver. They can be filled with batter and placed directly on a baking sheet. No muffin pan — no clean up.

Baking Stones — These aren't a necessity, but we love what they do for the crusts of yeast breads and pizzas. They hold the heat well and almost convert your stove to an old-fashioned brick oven. Treat them as directed by the manufacturer. Unglazed quarry tiles are available from lumberyards. Glazed tiles may contain lead and other unhealthy compounds.

Citrus Zesters and Peelers — Citrus zest can be removed with a box or flat, hand-held grater, with a zester (this is a wonderful tool), or even with a swivel vegetable peeler. In all cases, avoid removing the white pith just under the colored skin. If using a grater, cover it first with a piece of plastic wrap. You'll be able to recover a lot more zest and cleanup will be easier. If using a zester or peeler, both of which produce longer strips, chop the zest to the desired size after removing it from the fruit.

Cooling Racks — Large wire racks are essential baking tools. You can improvise with racks from discarded ovens or other appliances.

Deep-frying Equipment and Techniques — If you buy a deep fryer, look for one with adjustable heat control and a volume adequate to your needs. A big wok or wok-style skillet and a frying thermometer can easily be substituted. Oil or fat for deep frying (we generally prefer a neutral oil like canola) can be reused if strained, but we don't recommend this. Cooking often "burns" the oil, changing its flavor.

Food Processors, Blenders and Choppers — Life is a lot easier when you own one or more of these "hard working" appliances. We think a good food processor is the most functional of the three, if you have to make a choice. It's more powerful and versatile. Blenders often require the addition of some liquid, which is incompatible to many ingredients.

Ice Cream Maker — You don't need one, but having one is great fun, allowing you to make unusual and delicious ice creams, sherbets and fruit ices.

Knives — Use good quality knives that feel comfortable in your hand. A small paring knife and two larger slicing knives (one plain-bladed and one serrated) are the minimum. We also like to use a cleaver for chopping. Knives should be protected (don't use them as screwdrivers or scrapers) and kept sharp.

Measuring Tools — Although most recipes are a lot more forgiving than you may think, it is best to use calibrated measuring cups and spoons. For measuring small amounts of dry ingredients, we found the spoons and scoops with adjustable slides for different measures to be extremely handy. Don't use them for liquid ingredients, though.

Mixer — One of the best presents a cook can get is a heavy-duty stand mixer. Treat yourself — you deserve it. This versatile appliance makes mixing, whipping and kneading effortless. We'd be lost without our KitchenAid™ mixers.

Microwave Oven — Frankly, we didn't use a microwave once while testing these recipes. However, they are very good at melting butter and chocolate and reheating those lethal leftovers. (Buy the mixer instead.)

Mise en Place — Not a tool but a technique. Basically, it means preparing and setting out your ingredients before beginning to cook. For example, sift your dry ingredients, measure out your fruits or nuts, melt and measure your butter, grease your pans, etc., before you start mixing. It improves your product by reducing sitting time and also assures you will be less likely to leave something out.

Saucepans and Skillets — The best pans you can afford are the best investment. We prefer heavy stainless steel saucepans and skillets. A double boiler is very handy for delicate jobs like melting chocolate. You can improvise with two different size pots and a steamer rack.

Final Words

Buttermilk can be used in most recipes calling for sour milk, yogurt or sour cream. Just remember to compensate for the variances in texture and fluidity.

Recipes are only guidelines. Experiment. Substitute. Have fun. If it comes out good, tout our book. If it comes out badly, cover it with whipped cream.

Biscuits, Dumplings, Shortcakes & Cobblers

ABOUT BISCUITS

Unsweetened biscuits are a true "quick bread." Simply served hot with butter, used as a base or topping for stews or flavored with herbs or other ingredients, biscuits make every supper special.

Sweetened, these little breads can serve as a base for a myriad of desserts, limited only by the reaches of your imagination.

We vastly prefer biscuits made from scratch to the ones in the exploding tubes or biscuits made from the dry prepared mixes sold in supermarkets. Homemade biscuits are a lot less expensive and don't taste like the creation of a chemist working in a salt mine.

Most biscuits are leavened with baking powder and/or baking soda. A special and particularly light and luscious variety adds yeast, but you must remember to start them about an hour before you would the more common type.

If you have access to it, soft wheat flour specifically formulated for biscuits is an excellent choice. We make our yeast biscuits with regular all-purpose flour to take advantage of its higher gluten content. Our choice for "no-yeast" biscuits is a mixture of all-purpose and cake or pastry flour.

Following a few simple rules will assure a perfect batch of biscuits:

✓ Mix dry ingredients well to assure an even distribution of leavenings and seasonings.

✓ Knead only a few times, until the dough forms a coherent ball. Over-kneading makes biscuits tough.

✓ Don't roll or pat out too thinly. If you re-roll the scraps, do it only once. Expect your biscuits to rise a little more than double while baking.

✓ Use a biscuit cutter and avoid twisting the cutter during cutting or you will squash the edges and partially discourage rising.

✓ Make sure the oven has fully preheated before you begin baking.

✓ Biscuits freeze well. Reheat frozen biscuits in a 350° oven until warmed through.

ANGEL WING YEAST BISCUITS

1 Dozen Biscuits

Our testers said, "These are what biscuits should be." The dough can be made ahead of time and left in the refrigerator overnight. See BISCUIT ADDITIONS for variations.

1 package active dry yeast

1/4 cup lukewarm water

2-3/4 cups all-purpose flour

1/2 teaspoon baking soda

1 teaspoon baking powder

1 teaspoon salt

2 tablespoons sugar

1/2 cup vegetable shortening

1 cup room-temperature buttermilk

In a small bowl, dissolve yeast in warm water. Proof yeast (see page 120) until foamy, about 10 minutes.

In a large bowl, mix flour, baking soda, baking powder, salt and sugar. Cut in shortening until the mixture resembles coarse meal.

Add yeast and buttermilk, mixing well.

Turn out on a dry, floured surface. Knead about one minute. Dough will be soft and smooth. Pat dough out to 3/4" thickness.

Using a 2" biscuit cutter, cut out biscuits. Place 1" apart on an ungreased baking sheet. Cover biscuits with a towel and let rise 45 minutes.

Preheat oven to 400°

Bake 12 to 15 minutes on an ungreased baking sheet until light, golden brown.

> Although grandma may have cut her biscuits with a jelly glass, don't do it. It crimps the edges and your biscuits won't rise properly.

CONSENSUS NO-YEAST BISCUITS

8 Large Biscuits

1-1/2 cups all-purpose flour

1/2 cup cake flour

1 tablespoon baking powder

1/2 teaspoon baking soda

3/4 teaspoon salt

1/2 cup vegetable shortening

3/4 cup buttermilk

Preheat oven to 450°

Baking powder buttermilk biscuit recipes abound. We think we tested all of them! This recipe takes parts from all of the best. Our tasters passed on all the rest.

In a large mixing bowl, combine flours, baking powder, baking soda and salt. Cut in shortening until the mixture resembles coarse meal. Using a fork, mix in buttermilk just to moisten.

Turn dough out onto a dry, floured surface. Knead briefly — 5 to 6 turns, only. Pat dough out to 3/4" thickness.

Using a 2-1/2" biscuit cutter, cut out biscuits. Reroll scraps once and cut again. Place 1" apart on an ungreased baking sheet.

Bake 12 to 15 minutes until golden brown.

BISCUIT ADDITIONS & VARIATIONS

PEPPER BISCUITS:
Add 1 tablespoon coarsely ground pepper with dry ingredients. These make a good base for creamed chicken.

SUNSHINE BISCUITS:
Add 1 tablespoon grated citrus zest with dry ingredients.

BACON BLUE CHEESE BISCUITS:
Add 4 crumbled slices of crisp cooked bacon to the dry ingredients and cut in 1/4 cup crumbled blue cheese with the shortening.

DATE & NUT BISCUITS:
Add 1/2 cup finely diced dates and 1/3 cup chopped walnuts or pecans to mixture after cutting in the shortening.

HERB BISCUITS:
Add 1/4 cup minced fresh chives, dill, parsley or cilantro with dry ingredients.

WHOLE WHEAT BISCUITS:
Substitute 1/2 cup whole wheat flour for 1/2 cup of the all-purpose flour.

BEST RESTAURANT BISCUITS

We uncovered the secret ingredients — cheddar cheese and garlic butter — to the wonderful biscuits that are served at one of our local restaurants.

Garlic Butter:

At least 1 hour before baking biscuits, melt butter in a small saucepan. Stir in garlic. Remove from heat and let garlic steep until ready to bake.

Biscuits:

In a small bowl, dissolve yeast in warm water. Proof yeast (see page 120) until foamy, about 10 minutes.

In a large bowl, mix flour, baking soda, baking powder, salt and sugar. Cut in shortening and cheddar cheese until the mixture resembles coarse meal.

Add yeast and buttermilk, mixing well.

Turn out on a dry, floured surface. Knead about 1 minute. Dough will be soft and smooth. Pat dough out to 3/4" thickness.

Using a 2" biscuit cutter, cut out biscuits. Place 1" apart on an ungreased baking sheet. Cover biscuits with a towel and let rise 45 minutes.

Strain the minced garlic from the butter. Brush biscuits with butter.

Bake 12 to 15 minutes until light, golden brown.

Garlic Butter:
2 tablespoons butter
1 clove garlic, minced

Biscuits:
1 packet active dry yeast
1/4 cup lukewarm water
2-3/4 cups all-purpose flour
1/2 teaspoon baking soda
1 teaspoon baking powder
1-1/2 teaspoons salt
2 tablespoons sugar
1/2 cup vegetable shortening
1/2 cup grated cheddar cheese
1 cup room-temperature buttermilk

Preheat oven to 400°

Garlic butter can be stored in the refrigerator for several weeks. Brush it on bread or rolls and wrap them in foil leaving the bread partially exposed and bake at about 350° for about 15 minutes until warm and crisp. Voilà!…Garlic bread.

PESTO BISCUITS

1 Dozen Biscuits

2 cups all-purpose flour

1/2 cup cake flour

1 tablespoon baking powder

1/2 teaspoon baking soda

1/2 teaspoon salt

1/3 cup vegetable shortening

3 tablespoon pesto (see recipe below, or use commercially prepared pesto)

2/3 cup buttermilk

We love pesto and have included this recipe to show the versatility of our PESTO SAUCE. Serve these biscuits with soups or stews.

In a large bowl, combine flours, baking powder, baking soda and salt. Cut in shortening and pesto. Using a fork, mix in buttermilk just to moisten.

Turn dough out onto a dry, floured surface. Knead briefly — 5 to 6 turns only. Pat dough out to 3/4" thickness.

Using a 2" biscuit cutter, cut out biscuits. Place 1" apart on an ungreased baking sheet.

Bake 10 to 12 minutes until golden brown.

Preheat oven to 450°

PESTO SAUCE

2 Cups

1-1/2 cups tightly packed, fresh basil leaves

3 cloves garlic

1/4 cup freshly grated parmesan or romano cheese

1/2 cup extra-virgin olive oil

1/4 cup pine nuts or walnuts

salt and freshly ground pepper to taste

This recipe can be doubled, tripled and quadrupled depending on your supply of basil. Here in the northeast, we make it in big batches when basil is plentiful and freeze small quantities for wintertime biscuits, pizzas and sauces.

In a food processor, briefly process basil and garlic until basil is coarsely chopped. Add cheese and process to blend. With the motor running, slowly add the olive oil. Add the nuts and blend the mixture until smooth. Stir in salt and pepper.

> Cover unused pesto with a thin layer of olive oil to retard browning. Store in refrigerator or freeze.

6 Servings

Dumplings make every stew or fricassee special. Make the dough just before you are ready to cook the dumplings. Resist peeking in the pot. It toughens the dumplings.

In a medium-size mixing bowl, sift together the flour, baking powder, baking soda and salt. Cut in the shortening until the mixture resembles coarse meal. With a fork, mix in the buttermilk. The dough will be soft.

Drop dumplings by 1/4 cupfuls onto simmering (not boiling) stew. Try to place the dumplings on top of chunks of meat or vegetables. Cover and simmer for 15 minutes. Test for doneness with a toothpick. If the pick doesn't come out clean, continue simmering with the lid off for a couple of minutes.

2 cups all-purpose flour

1-1/2 teaspoons baking powder

1/2 teaspoon baking soda

1 teaspoon salt

1-1/2 tablespoons vegetable shortening

1 cup buttermilk

DUMPLING VARIATIONS

PARSLEY DUMPLINGS:
Add 1/4 cup chopped parsley with the dry ingredients.

CORNMEAL DUMPLINGS:
Substitute 1/2 cup cornmeal for 1/2 cup flour. Add 2 teaspoons sugar to dry ingredients.

HERB DUMPLINGS:
Add 2 tablespoons minced fresh or 2 teaspoons dried herbs to dry ingredients.

ONION DUMPLINGS:
Sauté 1/4 cup finely chopped onion in 2 teaspoons butter until slightly browned. Add to dry ingredients.

BACON DUMPLINGS:
Add 3 strips cooked, crisp, crumbled bacon to the dry ingredients.

PARMESAN DUMPLINGS:
Add 1/4 cup freshly grated parmesan cheese to dry ingredients.

CHEDDAR POPOVERS

6 Popovers

2 eggs
1/4 teaspoon salt
1 cup buttermilk
1 cup all-purpose
  flour
1/4 pound cheddar
  cheese, grated

Preheat oven to 450°

With so little effort, popovers always make a statement.

Grease 6 six-ounce custard cups well.

Beat the eggs briefly with the salt and milk. Beat gradually into the flour to make a smooth batter full of air bubbles. Stir in cheese.

Divide among prepared cups. Set on baking sheet.

Bake for 25 minutes, then reduce heat to 350° and bake for 15 minutes until brown, crisp and popped.

TO HEAT OR NOT TO HEAT...
THE POPOVER CONTROVERSY

Greased popover cups were traditionally heated before the batter was added. Newer recipes often suggest using unheated cups.

We tested both methods. The results were identical in both crispness and size.

BASIC SWEET BISCUIT DOUGH

Enough for 8 Biscuits or 1 Cobbler

This BASIC SWEET BISCUIT DOUGH is the basis for most of our shortcake and cobbler creations.

In a large mixing bowl, combine flour, sugar, baking powder and baking soda. Cut in butter until mixture resembles coarse meal. Gently toss in buttermilk until mixture barely forms a ball.

See ROLLED BISCUIT SHORTCAKES, DROP BISCUIT SHORTCAKES and COBBLER DOUGH for preparation and baking instructions.

1-1/4 cups all-purpose flour

2 tablespoons sugar

1-1/4 teaspoon baking powder

1/4 teaspoon baking soda

4 tablespoons chilled butter, in small pieces

1/2 cup buttermilk

ROLLED BISCUIT SHORTCAKES

Preheat oven to 425°

On a lightly floured surface, roll or pat the dough out 3/4" thick. Cut round biscuits with a biscuit cutter, patting together scraps to form more biscuits, or form square biscuits by cutting the dough with a knife. Too much rolling or working of the dough will toughen it, so don't be a slave to form.

Brush with melted butter or buttermilk. Sprinkle with sugar. Place on a greased baking sheet.

Bake 15 minutes until golden.

DROP BISCUIT SHORTCAKES

Preheat oven to 425°

Drop dough by 1/4 cupfuls onto a greased baking sheet. Brush with melted butter or buttermilk. Sprinkle with sugar.

Bake 15 minutes until golden.

COBBLER DOUGH for One 9" x 13" Cobbler

See various cobbler recipes for oven temperatures

Strew scrap-size (scant 1/4 cupfuls) portions on top of the cobbler base, leaving small space between scraps for steam to escape. If you prefer to roll the cobbler crust, cut vents for steam.

APPLE SHORTCAKE with WARM LEMON SAUCE

10 Shortcakes

Apple filling:
2 cups water
1 cup sugar
6 tart apples
1/2 cup raisins
1/2 cup walnuts

Sauce:
1/2 cup sugar
1 tablespoon
  cornstarch
zest of one lemon
1 cup cold water
2 tablespoons butter,
  cut in small pieces

All of the parts of this dessert can be made ahead. The lemon sauce should be reheated on low before assembling the shortcakes.

Prepare and bake a SWEET BISCUIT DOUGH (ROLLED OR DROPPED BISCUIT SHORTCAKES) recipe.

Filling:

In a medium saucepan, stir the sugar into the water. Cook over medium heat for about 5 minutes until sugar is totally dissolved.

In the meantime, peel, core and slice apples. Poach apples and raisins in the hot syrup until apples are tender. Drain and cool. Reserve syrup.

Sauce:

In a medium saucepan, combine sugar, cornstarch, and lemon zest and water. Cook, stirring constantly until thickened. Swirl in butter.

Assembly:

Stir walnuts into cooled apple mixture. Add enough reserved syrup to moisten. Layer shortcake with apple mixture. Top with warm sauce.

BANANAS FOSTER SHORTCAKE

10 Shortcakes

Prepare and bake a SWEET BISCUIT DOUGH (ROLLED OR DROPPED BISCUIT SHORTCAKES) recipe.

In a heavy skillet, sauté banana slices in butter until golden. Stir in brown sugar and cinnamon, stirring gently until brown sugar has melted. Remove from heat. Add rum, return to heat and cook 1 minute.

Split biscuits and place on individual plates. Top with banana slices and whipped cream.

1/2 cup butter
6 large bananas, sliced
1/2 teaspoon cinnamon
3/4 cup brown sugar
6 tablespoons rum
2 cups sweetened whipped cream or crème fraîche

CHOCOLATE SHORTCAKE DROP BISCUITS

12 Biscuits

Grease a baking sheet or line with parchment paper.

In a large mixing bowl, combine flour, cocoa, sugar, baking powder, baking soda and salt.

In a separate, small mixing bowl, mix egg, buttermilk and zest (see page xvii).

Cut the butter into dry ingredients until mixture resembles coarse meal.

Add the egg mixture and stir until just moistened. Dough will be soft.

Drop by 1/4 cupfuls on prepared baking sheet. Sprinkle with sugar. Bake for 20 minutes or until biscuits test done. Transfer to a wire rack to cool.

2-1/2 cups all-purpose flour
1/4 cup cocoa
1/2 cup sugar
1 teaspoon baking powder
1/2 teaspoon baking soda
1/2 teaspoon salt
1 egg, beaten
3/4 cup cold buttermilk
2 teaspoons orange zest
3/4 cup cold butter, cut in small pieces
sugar for sprinkling

Preheat oven to 400°

GINGER PEAR SHORTCAKE with GINGER CUSTARD SAUCE

10 Shortcakes

Pear filling:

2 cups water

1 cup sugar

1" piece fresh ginger, peeled and cut lengthwise

6 firm, ripe pears

Custard Sauce:

2 cups buttermilk

4 egg yolks

1/2 cup sugar

1-1/2 teaspoons vanilla

1/4 teaspoon ground ginger

Prepare and bake a SWEET BISCUIT DOUGH (ROLLED OR DROPPED BISCUIT SHORTCAKES) recipe.

Filling:

In a medium saucepan, stir the sugar into the water. Add ginger. Cook over medium heat for about 5 minutes until sugar is totally dissolved.

Meanwhile, peel, core and slice pears. Poach pears in the hot syrup until tender. Drain and cool.

Custard Sauce:

In a medium saucepan, whisk together milk, yolks, and sugar. Over medium flame, heat the mixture slowly, stirring constantly, until the mixture coats the back of the spoon. Do not allow mixture to boil. Remove from heat. Stir in vanilla and ground ginger. Use immediately or cover surface with wax paper and serve at room temperature later.

Assembly:

Split shortcakes. Layer with poached pears. Top with custard sauce.

> Candied ginger is a good emergency substitute for fresh gingerroot. Ground dried ginger has a different taste and should not be used in place of fresh ginger.

BLUEBERRY COBBLER

9" Square Cobbler

Butter a 9" square pan.

Place 2 cups blueberries in medium saucepan. Mash coarsely with potato masher. Stir in sugar and cinnamon. Mix cornstarch, lemon juice and water until smooth. Stir into berries. Stir over medium heat until mixture clears and thickens slightly. Stir in remaining 2 cups of berries and continue cooking 5 minutes. Pour into prepared pan.

Top with cobbler dough as directed. Bake 15 to 20 minutes until golden.

4 cups fresh or thawed frozen blueberries, divided

1/2 cup sugar

1 teaspoon cinnamon

1 tablespoon cornstarch

1 teaspoon lemon juice

1 tablespoon water

1 recipe BASIC SWEET BISCUIT DOUGH

Preheat oven to 425°

> *Working with cornstarch:* Cornstarch is a good thickener for fruit cobblers and has an attractive glossy finish. Unless otherwise directed, cornstarch should be mixed with a cold liquid to form a slurry before being heated to avoid lumps. A fruit mixture with cornstarch will initially be cloudy. After it reaches the boiling point, the mixture will clear and become shiny. If you are out of cornstarch, substitute about twice the volume of flour. Potato starch or arrowroot, while good thickeners, will not stand up to baking.

BRANDIED APPLE COBBLER

9" x 13" Cobbler

6 cups peeled, sliced
  tart apples

3/4 cup dark brown
  sugar

1 teaspoon cinnamon

1/4 teaspoon freshly
  grated nutmeg

1/2 cup raisins or
  currants

1/4 cup brandy

1/4 cup melted butter

1 recipe BASIC
  SWEET BISCUIT
  DOUGH

This grown-up version of apple cobbler is especially good served warm with vanilla ice cream.

Butter a 9" x 13" baking pan.

Toss apples with brown sugar, cinnamon, nutmeg and raisins until well coated. Turn into prepared pan. Mix brandy and butter. Drizzle evenly over apples. Bake fruit 20 minutes. Remove from oven.

Cover fruit with dough. Return to oven and bake 20 minutes until golden.

Preheat oven to 400°

DOUBLE CHERRY COBBLER

9" Square Cobbler

Fresh, frozen or canned unsweetened cherries can be used in this dessert.

Butter a 9" square pan.

In a medium saucepan, mix sugar and cornstarch. Stir in water. Add cherries. Cook and stir over medium heat until mixture clears and thickens. Remove from heat. Stir in almond extract, butter and dried cherries. Cover fruit with dough. Sprinkle with almonds, pressing lightly with fingertips. Bake 15 to 20 minutes until golden.

2/3 cup sugar

2 tablespoons cornstarch

3/4 cup water

3 cups tart or sweet cherries

1/4 teaspoon almond extract

1 tablespoon butter

1/2 cup dried cherries

1 recipe BASIC SWEET BISCUIT DOUGH

1/4 cup slivered almonds

Preheat oven to 425°

PRALINE PEACH COBBLER

9" x 13" Cobbler

1-1/2 cups sugar

2 tablespoons
cornstarch

1 teaspoon cinnamon

1 cup water

8 cups sliced, peeled
fresh or frozen
peaches

3 tablespoons melted
butter

1/4 cup dark brown
sugar

1 cup pecans, chopped

1 recipe BASIC
SWEET BISCUIT
DOUGH

Preheat oven to 400°

A little out of the ordinary.

Butter a 9" x 13" baking pan.

In large saucepan, combine sugar, cornstarch, cinnamon and water. Bring to boil. Add peaches. Return to boil and simmer 5 minutes, stirring constantly. Pour mixture into prepared pan.

Mix butter and brown sugar. Add pecans. Sprinkle over fruit. Cover fruit with dough. Bake 20 to 25 minutes until lightly browned.

Pancakes, Waffles & French Toast

PANCAKES, WAFFLES & FRENCH TOAST

There is something very nurturing about serving and eating homemade pancakes, waffles and French toast. And remember, they're not just for breakfast.

Cook extra to freeze for all the convenience of store-bought at a fraction of the cost. Cool cooked pancakes, waffles or French toast completely. Separate individual pieces with wax paper and store airtight in the freezer up to two months. To reheat, place frozen pieces on a baking sheet and bake at 350° until heated through, or pop them in the toaster.

The first pancake is a test. If it browns too quickly, lower the heat. If it's pale, but cooked through, raise the heat slightly. Plan on throwing the first one out or serve it to whomever is nudging your elbow.

Hold cooked pancakes in 200° oven while preparing the rest.

Waffle batter spreads in the waffle iron. Pour in just enough batter to cover 3/4 of the iron's surface.

BASIC BUTTERMILK PANCAKES

About 8 Pancakes

A most alluring illusion — they aren't really floating above the plate!

See PANCAKE VARIATIONS and PANCAKE, WAFFLE & FRENCH TOAST TOPPINGS for tasty suggestions.

Mix flour, salt and baking soda. Add egg, oil, vanilla, sugar and buttermilk. Stir just until combined. Batter will be slightly lumpy.

Drop by 1/4 cupfuls onto hot greased griddle or skillet, spreading slightly with back of a spoon. Cook over medium-low heat until edges begin to dry and surface bubbles pop. Flip and brown on other side.

1 cup all-purpose flour

1/4 teaspoon salt

1 teaspoon baking soda

1 egg

2 tablespoons vegetable oil or melted butter

1 teaspoon vanilla extract

1 tablespoon sugar (optional)

1 cup buttermilk

PANCAKE VARIATIONS

BANANA WALNUT PANCAKES:
Add 1 diced ripe banana and 1/4 cup chopped walnuts to batter.

BLUEBERRY PANCAKES:
Sprinkle each pancake with about 2 tablespoons fresh or unthawed frozen blueberries immediately after spreading in pan. You can mix the berries into the batter if desired, but frozen berries may bleed and turn the batter purple.

FAMILY RAISIN PANCAKES:
Add 1/2 cup raisins to batter.

ADULT RAISIN PANCAKES:
Plump 1/2 cup raisins in 2 tablespoons orange flavored liqueur. Add undrained raisins to batter.

STRAWBERRY PANCAKES:
Add 3/4 cup sliced fresh or frozen unsweetened strawberries to batter.

PINEAPPLE PANCAKES:
Add 1/2 cup well-drained crushed pineapple to batter.

APPLE OVEN PANCAKE

6 to 8 Servings

2 apples, peeled and thinly sliced

2 teaspoons cinnamon

1/2 cup sugar

1/4 cup dark brown sugar

3/4 cup all-purpose flour

1 teaspoon baking powder

1/8 teaspoon salt

3/4 cup buttermilk

3 eggs, lightly beaten

2 tablespoons vegetable oil

5 tablespoons butter

With a baked pancake, the cook doesn't have to stand over the pan with a spatula.

Lightly oil bottom and sides of a 10" ovenproof skillet.

Mix apples, cinnamon and sugars. Set aside.

Mix flour, baking powder and salt. Stir in buttermilk, eggs and oil just to moisten. Melt butter in prepared skillet. Add apple mixture. Stir over medium-low heat until sugars are melted, about 5 minutes. Spread apple mixture evenly in pan. Pour batter over apples.

Bake until puffed and lightly browned, about 25 to 35 minutes. Cut in wedges and serve hot.

Preheat oven to 375°

BUTTERMILK WAFFLES

4 to 6 Servings

2 egg whites

1-1/2 cups all-purpose flour

3 teaspoons baking powder

1/4 teaspoon baking soda

2 teaspoons sugar

2 egg yolks, beaten

1-1/4 cups buttermilk

3 tablespoons melted butter

Crispy and warm with little pools of melted butter. What could be better?

Beat egg whites until stiff. Set aside.

Sift together flour, baking powder, baking soda and sugar. In a large mixing bowl, combine dry ingredients with egg yolks, buttermilk and butter. Gently fold in egg whites. Add more milk if necessary to form a thin batter.

Bake in waffle iron according to manufacturer's instructions.

BLUEBERRY CORNMEAL PANCAKES

8 to 10 Cakes

Good taste, great texture. Terrific topped with LEMON BLUEBERRY SAUCE.

Mix cornmeal, flour, salt, sugar, baking soda and lemon zest. Stir in butter, eggs, buttermilk and blueberries.

Heat lightly greased skillet over medium-low heat. Drop batter by slightly heaping 1/4 cupfuls into skillet. Tilt to spread batter. Cook until dry and beginning to brown around bottom edges. Turn and brown other side.

1 cup cornmeal

1/2 cup all-purpose flour

1/2 teaspoon salt

1 tablespoon sugar

1 teaspoon baking soda

1 teaspoon lemon zest

1 tablespoon melted butter

2 beaten eggs

1 cup buttermilk

1 cup fresh blueberries

BUTTERMILK FRENCH TOAST

4 Servings

DAIRY CHALLAH BREAD makes the best French toast.

In a wide soup bowl, beat together eggs, buttermilk, sugar, vanilla and cinnamon. Dip both side of bread slices into egg mixture.

Melt butter in skillet over medium-low heat.

Fry, turning once, until golden on both sides.

2 beaten eggs

1/2 cup buttermilk

1 tablespoon sugar

1/2 teaspoon vanilla extract

1/4 teaspoon cinnamon (optional)

4 thick slices of bread

butter for frying

CHOCOLATE WAFFLES, PLEASE...

4 to 6 Servings

1/4 cup melted butter

1/2 cup cocoa

3/4 cup sugar

2 eggs, beaten

1 teaspoon vanilla
extract

1 cup all-purpose
flour

1/2 teaspoon baking
soda

1/2 teaspoon salt

1/2 cup buttermilk

3/4 cup chopped
walnuts (optional)

The ultimate fun food! Serve with ice cream, whipped cream or chocolate sauce.

These also make good ice cream sandwiches. Just fill with softened ice cream and pop in the freezer.

Mix butter, cocoa and sugar well. Beat in eggs and vanilla. Add flour, baking soda, salt and walnuts alternately with buttermilk, stirring just to moisten. Batter will be thick.

Bake in a waffle iron according to manufacturer's instructions.

EASY CORN WAFFLES

4 to 6 Servings

1-1/2 cups cornmeal

1/3 cup all-purpose
flour

1 teaspoon baking
soda

2 tablespoons sugar

2 cups buttermilk

1/4 cup melted butter
or vegetable oil

1 egg, beaten

1 cup fresh or frozen
corn kernels

These waffles are sure to become one of your most requested breakfast or easy supper treats. For a change of flavor, omit the corn kernels and substitute 1/2 cup dried cherries or raisins and a little cinnamon.

Mix cornmeal, flour, baking soda and sugar. Add buttermilk, butter and egg. Stir just until moistened.

Bake in a waffle iron according to manufacturer's instructions.

Serve hot with butter and syrup or use as a base for savory stews.

MULTI-GRAIN PANCAKES

12 Pancakes

Made with wholesome grains, the molasses and honey provide just enough sweetness to make these good-for-you pancakes good-to-eat.

Mix flours, baking powder, baking soda and salt. Add buttermilk, molasses and honey. Mix just until blended.

Heat lightly greased skillet over medium-low flame. Drop batter by slightly heaping 1/4 cupfuls into skillet. Tilt to spread batter. Cook until dry and beginning to brown around bottom edges. Turn and brown other side.

Serve hot with butter and syrup.

3/4 cup rye flour
1/2 cup whole wheat flour
1/4 cup all-purpose flour
1 teaspoon baking powder
1/2 teaspoon baking soda
1/2 teaspoon salt
2 cups buttermilk
2 tablespoons molasses
2 tablespoons honey

OLD-FASHIONED OATMEAL RAISIN PANCAKES

9 Large Pancakes

The comforting smell of warm cinnamon and raisins will make you forget there's a cold morning outside. We like these spread with CINNAMON HONEY BUTTER.

Mix oatmeal and buttermilk. Let sit 20 minutes. Beat in egg, butter and sugar. Sift flour with baking powder, baking soda, cinnamon and salt. Stir into oatmeal mixture just to moisten. Stir in raisins. Let stand 15 minutes.

Heat lightly greased skillet over medium-low flame. Drop batter by slightly heaping 1/4 cupfuls into skillet. Tilt to spread batter. Cook until dry and beginning to brown around bottom edges. Turn and brown other side.

1 cup quick-cooking oatmeal
1 cup buttermilk
1 egg, beaten
1/8 cup melted cooled butter
1 tablespoon sugar
1/4 cup all-purpose flour
1/2 teaspoon baking powder
1/2 teaspoon baking soda
1/4 teaspoon cinnamon
1/4 teaspoon salt
1/4 cup raisins

ORANGE GINGERBREAD PANCAKES

About 8 Pancakes

1 cup all-purpose
flour

1/2 teaspoon salt

1/2 teaspoon baking
soda

3/4 teaspoon baking
powder

1 teaspoon cinnamon

2 teaspoons ground
ginger

3/4 teaspoon freshly
grated nutmeg

1 cup buttermilk

2 tablespoons
molasses

1 tablespoon sugar

1 large egg, beaten

1 tablespoon melted
butter

grated zest of 1 small
orange

1 tablespoon fresh
orange juice

Don't let the long list of ingredients intimidate you. This recipe is a snap and the pancakes have the real bite of gingerbread! Serve with ORANGE BUTTER and warm maple syrup.

Mix flour, salt, baking soda, baking powder, cinnamon, ginger and nutmeg. Set aside.

In a medium bowl, mix buttermilk, molasses, sugar, egg, butter, orange zest and orange juice. Stir in dry ingredients just until completely moistened.

Drop batter by 1/4 cupfuls on hot, greased griddle or skillet, tilting to spread slightly. Cook over medium-low heat until edges begin to dry. There won't be as many bubbles as with an ordinary batter. Flip and brown on other side. These can burn easily.

PANCAKE, WAFFLE & FRENCH TOAST TOPPINGS

BERRY PEACH TOPPING

Of course, in-season fresh fruits can be substituted, but we find we especially crave their sweet goodness after the frost sets in.

Combine all ingredients. Cover and let stand at room temperature about one hour.

1-pound bag frozen sliced peaches

12-ounce bag frozen blackberries

1/4 cup honey

1/2 teaspoon ground cardamom

CINNAMON HONEY BUTTER

Cream all ingredients together until smooth and pale in color. Keeps well, tightly covered in the refrigerator.

1/2 cup best quality honey

1/2 pound butter at room temperature

1/4 teaspoon cinnamon

LEMON BLUEBERRY SAUCE

This sauce can be made several days ahead. It keeps well in the refrigerator if someone doesn't snitch it to top their ice cream.

In a heavy saucepan, combine all ingredients. Stir constantly over medium heat until sugar dissolves. Bring to a boil, stirring occasionally, until mixture thickens.

1 pound fresh or frozen blueberries

1/2 cup sugar

zest of one large lemon

2 teaspoons cornstarch mixed with juice of 1 large lemon

ORANGE BUTTER

Cream all ingredients together.

2 teaspoons frozen orange juice concentrate, thawed

1/2 cup butter

1/2 teaspoon freshly grated ginger

More Toppings

SPICED HONEY PLUMS

2 cups light cream

3 tablespoons
  buttermilk

4 tablespoons honey

2 pounds sliced ripe
  fresh, frozen or
  canned plums

1/4 to 1/2 cup sugar,
  depending on
  sweetness of the fruit

1/4 teaspoon
  cinnamon

*Prepare the cream-honey mixture for this
topping the night before.*

Whisk together cream, buttermilk and honey.
Set aside for several hours at room
temperature or overnight in refrigerator until
thickened.

While your pancakes or waffles are cooking,
place plums and sugar in a large skillet over
medium heat. Stir constantly until sugar
dissolves and plums are glazed and tender.
Sprinkle with cinnamon. Combine with cream
mixture.

TROPICAL TOPPING

1 cup sweetened
  flaked coconut

1 fresh pineapple,
  cubed

1 sliced banana

3 kiwi fruit, peeled
  and cubed

1 small mango, peeled
  and cubed

juice of one lime

1/2 cup dark brown
  sugar

Toss ingredients together. Let stand at room
temperature about one hour to exude juices.

Cakes & Frostings

ABOUT CAKES

The introduction of cake mixes after World War II dramatically changed the role of cakes in home cooking. Before mid-century, a cook was often judged by the quality of his or her cakes. Cake was a fairly common everyday dessert and, of course, there were a wide variety of fancy cakes suited to special occasions.

Why make cakes from scratch when every grocery store has shelves full of cake mixes and a ready supply of even less demanding frozen and prepared products?

☞ Because your cake won't taste like salt, artificial flavorings or the box it came in.

☞ Because your cakes won't contain propylene glycol monoesters (the stuff they spray on airplanes to remove ice) and sodium aluminum phosphate (which would rot steel), and they won't have a shelf life measured in years.

☞ Because your cakes will be different and better than everyone else's.

☞ Because you'll be proud of your accomplishments.

☞ Because it's almost as easy as emptying a box.

GOOD CAKE RULES

✓ Sift dry ingredients to assure a good distribution of leavening agents.

✓ If the recipe specifies cake flour, sift it before measuring. To substitute all-purpose flour for cake flour on a cup-for-cup basis, remove 2 tablespoons all-purpose flour from the cup, add 2 tablespoons cornstarch and sift together.

✓ Softened butter is butter left sitting out until it comes to room temperature. Heating or microwaving butter to soften it will dramatically alter the cake's texture. If you've forgotten to set out the butter and absolutely have to proceed, chop it into fine bits before creaming.

✓ Cream butter and sugar mixtures very well. The mixture should not have a grainy texture.

✓ Unless otherwise specified, beat in eggs one at a time.

✓ Unless otherwise specified, beat completed batter at least three minutes to incorporate air.

✓ Prepare baking pans as directed. If the cake needs to be turned out of the baking pan, grease the pan, line the bottom with a circle of parchment or wax paper slightly smaller than the circumference of the pan, grease the paper and dust the bottom and sides with flour (or, if you prefer, cocoa for chocolate cakes).

✓ Spread the batter evenly. But remember, uneven cakes usually mean your oven is not completely level or heats unevenly.

✓ Make sure your oven is completely preheated before baking. If possible, use an oven thermometer to test the accuracy of your oven.

✓ If you need to use multiple oven racks to bake, rotate the pans about halfway through baking.

✓ Use suggested baking times only as a guide. There are several tests for doneness, including inserting picks to check for crumbs. We prefer to lightly touch the center of the cakes. They should feel firm and slightly springy. The cake should shrink slightly away from the sides of the pan.

✓ Cool cakes in their pans on a wire rack 5 to 10 minutes after removing them from the oven to allow the cakes to firm slightly. Then turn them out onto wire racks to cool completely, peeling off the paper. If too much time has passed and the cakes threaten to stay in the pans, return them to the still-warm oven for a few minutes and repeat the turning out process.

✓ Unless otherwise directed, cool cakes completely before filling and frosting.

✓ Cakes may be frozen, preferably unfrosted.

LAYER CAKES LESSONS

✓ Use a pastry brush to wipe away loose crumbs from the sides, edges and surfaces of cakes before applying any frosting.

✓ Place first layer right side up on serving plate. If presentation is a concern, tuck torn pieces of wax paper around the bottom of the cake to protect the plate from frosting drips. Fill the cake with filling or frosting. As an extra treat, sprinkle the cake layers with a flavored liqueur and/or spread with preserves before filling. Add layers, finishing with the final layer upside down so the cake is flat on top.

✓ A small metal spatula is especially handy for spreading frosting on the sides of cakes. Some of them have scalloped edges that will make an interesting design.

✓ Plan to let the frosted cake sit at least an hour, if possible, before serving to firm the icing.

✓ Cover frosted or unfrosted cakes for short-term storage.

ABOUT FROSTINGS and CONFECTIONS

Uncooked frostings, icings and candies pose few problems. Just remember to add liquids gradually. Simply add a little more sugar or liquid to arrive at the right consistency.

Working with cooked sugar can be tricky, but the results are usually worth the anxiety. A good candy thermometer is worth the investment. Test the thermometer by placing it in boiling water. It should read 212° Fahrenheit or 100° Celsius. Take care not to go beyond that point of no return where the mixture will never spread and requires a chisel to get it out of the pan. You can salvage a near-disaster by beating more buttermilk or confectioners sugar into the mixture. If it feels and tastes good by the fingerful, it will be just fine on the cake. If all else fails, console yourself by using it for an ice-cream topping.

PEACHY RYAN'S BLUEBERRY KUCHEN

9" x 13" Cake

This is one of those cakes that disappears before the oven cools.

Grease and flour a 9" x 13" baking pan.

Topping:

Prepare topping by mixing together sugar, flour and cinnamon. Cut in butter until mixture resembles coarse meal. Stir in pecans. Set aside.

Cake:

In a small mixing bowl, combine buttermilk, lemon zest, lemon juice and vanilla. Set aside.

In a large mixing bowl, cream together butter and sugar. Beat in eggs, one at a time.

Sift together flour, baking powder, baking soda, nutmeg and salt.

Combine creamed mixture with buttermilk mixture and dry ingredients, mixing just until moistened. Fold in 1 cup blueberries.

Spread batter in prepared pan. Top with 2 cups blueberries. Sprinkle on topping mixture.

Bake 40 to 45 minutes or until cake tests done.

Cool in pan on a wire rack.

Topping:

1/4 cup dark brown sugar
1 tablespoon all-purpose flour
1 teaspoon cinnamon
2 tablespoons softened butter
1 cup finely chopped pecans or walnuts

Cake:

1 cup buttermilk
1 teaspoon lemon zest
2 tablespoons lemon juice
1 teaspoon vanilla extract
6 tablespoons softened butter
3/4 cup sugar
2 eggs
2 cups all-purpose flour
1 teaspoon baking powder
1 teaspoon baking soda
1/2 teaspoon freshly grated nutmeg
1/4 teaspoon salt
3 cups fresh or unthawed frozen blueberries, divided

Preheat over to 325°

COCA-COLA® CAKE with COCA-COLA® ICING

9" x 13" Cake

Cake:

1 cup butter

1 cup Coca-Cola®

3 tablespoons cocoa

2 cups sugar

2 cups flour

1 teaspoon baking soda

2 eggs

1/2 cup buttermilk

1 teaspoon vanilla extract

1-1/2 cups miniature marshmallows

Icing:

1/2 cup butter

3 tablespoons unsweetened cocoa

6 tablespoons Coca-Cola®

1 pound confectioners sugar (1 box)

1 cup chopped walnuts

1 teaspoon vanilla extract

Preheat oven to 350°

We'd be remiss if we didn't include this "Classic Coke" recipe. No buttermilk primer would be complete without it. Warning: This cake is very sweet!

Cake:

Grease and flour a 9" x 13" baking pan.

In a medium-size saucepan, bring butter, cola and cocoa to a boil. Remove from heat.

In a large mixing bowl, combine sugar, flour, and baking soda. Add eggs, one at a time, beating well after each addition. Stir in buttermilk, vanilla, marshmallows and cola mixture. Beat well. The marshmallows will float.

Pour into prepared pan. Bake for 35 minutes until cake tests done.

Icing:

In a medium-size saucepan, bring butter, cocoa and cola to a boil. Stir in confectioners sugar. Stir in nuts and vanilla.

Spread on hot cake.

Some cooks substitute Dr. Pepper® or, of course, Pepsi-Cola®.

CRANBERRY LIME CAKE

10" Tube Cake

Prepare this cake the night before to give the tartness of the lime a chance to mellow. If you serve this before it has rested, you do so at your own risk! The festive color of the cranberries combined with the luscious lime overtones makes this a real celebration cake.

Grease and flour a 10" bundt or tube pan.

Cream together butter and sugar. Beat in eggs. Sift together flour, baking soda, baking powder and salt. Add dry ingredients to creamed mixture alternately with buttermilk. Beat well. Stir in lime zest, cranberries and pecans.

Pour into prepared pan.

Bake about 50 minutes or until cake tests done.

Meanwhile, prepare the syrup: In a small saucepan, over low heat, cook sugar and lime juice, stirring occasionally until sugar is dissolved. Set aside.

Cool cake in pan on wire rack 15 minutes. With a skewer, poke holes all over top of cake. Pour on warm syrup. Let sit in pan overnight to absorb syrup. Turn out.

Cake:
1/4 cup softened butter
1 cup sugar
2 eggs
2-1/4 cups all-purpose flour
1 teaspoon baking soda
1 teaspoon baking powder
1/4 teaspoon salt
1 cup buttermilk
4 teaspoons grated lime zest
2 cups whole fresh or frozen cranberries
1 cup chopped toasted pecans

Syrup:
3/4 cup fresh lime juice
1 cup sugar

Preheat oven to 350°

EVERYDAY CHOCOLATE CAKE

9" x 13" Cake

1-3/4 cups cake flour

3/4 cup cocoa

1-1/4 teaspoons baking soda

1/4 teaspoon salt

3/4 cup softened butter

2/3 cup granulated sugar

2/3 cup dark brown sugar

2 eggs

1-1/2 cups buttermilk

2 teaspoons vanilla extract

Grease and flour a 9" x 13" baking pan.

In a separate bowl, sift together flour, cocoa, baking soda and salt.

In a large mixing bowl, cream together butter, granulated and brown sugars. Add eggs one at a time, mixing well after each addition. Mix in flour mixture, alternately with buttermilk. Add vanilla. Beat well.

Pour batter into prepared pan. Bake for 25 to 30 minutes until cake tests done. Cool completely before frosting.

Frost with SHEET CAKE CHOCOLATE FROSTING.

Preheat oven to 350°

9" Layer Cake

This cake has a spectacular golden color. Frosted with CARAMEL FROSTING, it is as pretty to look at as it is good to eat.

Grease and flour two 9" layer cake pans.

In a large mixing bowl, cream together butter, granulated and brown sugars. Add eggs, one at a time, beating well after each addition.

Sift together flour, baking powder, baking soda, salt, cinnamon, allspice, cloves, nutmeg and cardamom. Add dry ingredients to creamed mixture alternately with buttermilk. Beat well.

Pour into prepared pans. Bake 45 minutes or until cake tests done. Cool in pans 10 minutes on wire rack. Turn out and cool completely.

Frost with CARAMEL FROSTING.

1/2 cup softened butter
1 cup granulated sugar
3/4 cup dark brown sugar
3 eggs
2-1/2 cups all-purpose flour
1 teaspoon baking powder
1 teaspoon baking soda
1 teaspoon salt
3/4 teaspoon cinnamon
3/4 teaspoon allspice
1/2 teaspoon cloves
1/2 teaspoon freshly grated nutmeg
1/4 teaspoon cardamom
1/2 cup buttermilk

Preheat oven to 350°

JELLY CUPBOARD CAKE

10" Tube Cake

3/4 cup soft butter

2 cups sugar

4 eggs

3 cups all-purpose flour

1 teaspoon baking soda

1/2 teaspoon ground allspice

1/2 teaspoon cinnamon

1/2 teaspoon freshly grated nutmeg

1 cup buttermilk

1/2 teaspoon vanilla extract

2/3 cup cherry preserves

2/3 cup peach or apricot preserves

2/3 cup pineapple preserves

1-1/2 cups pecans

Preheat oven to 325°

This mildly spiced fruit cake is very moist. Dust cooled cake with sifted confectioners sugar or a thin FRUIT GLAZE.

Grease and flour a 10" bundt or tube pan.

Cream together butter and sugar. Beat in eggs one at a time, beating well after each addition.

Sift flour, baking soda, allspice, cinnamon and nutmeg together. Add dry ingredients to creamed mixture alternately with buttermilk and vanilla. Beat well.

Stir in preserves. Fold in nuts.

Pour into prepared pan. Bake 1 1/2 hours until cake tests done. Cool in pan about 15 minutes. Loosen sides with a thin knife if necessary and turn out onto a wire rack to cool completely.

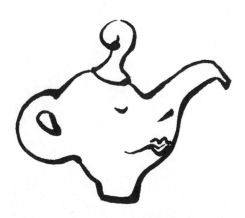

NOT YOUR NEIGHBOR'S CARROT CAKE

10" Tube or Three-layer Cake

The batter for this nouveau carrot cake makes a striking three-layer cake or one big, beautiful bundt cake.

Grease and flour a 10" tube or bundt pan, or three 9" cake pans.

Peel and coarsely chop carrots. Place in a medium-size saucepan with enough water to cover. Boil until very tender, about 1/2 hour. Drain.

In a blender or food processor, puree carrots with buttermilk.

In a large mixing bowl, combine carrot mixture with sugar, eggs and ginger. Mix in butter, vanilla and zest. Sift in flour, cinnamon, ginger and salt. Beat until combined. Stir in coconut.

Pour batter into prepared pan(s).

Bake for about 30 minutes until cake(s) tests done. Cool 10 minutes in pan on wire rack. Invert cake(s) onto wire racks and cool completely.

Frost layer cake with CREAM CHEESE FROSTING spiked with 1/4 cup minced, candied ginger and 1 teaspoon ground ginger.

The bundt cake is pretty enough to stand on its own.

1 pound carrots
  (about 3 large)
3/4 cup buttermilk
2 cups sugar
4 eggs
3 tablespoon minced,
  candied ginger
3/4 cup butter, melted
1 teaspoon vanilla
  extract
zest of one orange
3 cups all purpose
  flour
1 teaspoon cinnamon
1 teaspoon ground
  ginger
1 teaspoon salt
1/2 cup flaked coconut

Preheat oven to 350°

OAXACA CHOCOLATE CAKE

9" Layer Cake

4 ounces unsweetened chocolate

1/2 cup butter

2 cups sugar

2 eggs

1 teaspoon vanilla extract

2 cups cake flour

1 teaspoon baking soda

1/2 teaspoon baking powder

1 teaspoon salt

1 teaspoon cinnamon

3/4 cup hot water

3/4 cup buttermilk

Preheat oven to 350°

A friend from the Oaxaca region of Mexico suggested adding cinnamon to this otherwise simple chocolate cake.

In a double boiler, melt chocolate. Set aside to cool.

Grease two 9" cake pans. Line with parchment or wax paper. Grease the paper (**this is important**). Flour the pans.

In a large mixer bowl, cream together butter and sugar. Add eggs, one at a time, beating well after each addition. Stir in vanilla.

Sift together flour, baking soda, baking powder, salt and cinnamon.

Add dry ingredients, alternately with water and buttermilk to creamed mixture. Beat on low 30 seconds, scraping sides. Beat well. Stir in chocolate, mixing well.

Pour batter into pans and bake 30 to 35 minutes, until cake tests done. Cool 10 minutes, then turn out, peel off paper and cool on a wire rack.

Fill and frost cake with CREAMY CHOCOLATE FROSTING.

PEACH MOLASSES UPSIDE-DOWN CAKE

8" Square Cake

A very pretty presentation of a classic gingerbread cake.

Heavily grease an 8" square baking pan.

Arrange frozen peach slices in bottom of pan in a decorative pattern. Sprinkle peaches evenly with brown sugar.

Cream together butter, sugar and molasses. Sift flour with baking soda, ginger and cinnamon. Add dry ingredients alternately with buttermilk to creamed mixture. Beat well.

Drop batter by heaping tablespoons evenly over peaches. Spread carefully, taking care not to disturb peaches.

Bake 55 to 60 minutes until cake springs back when lightly touched.

Let cool in pan no more than 5 minutes. Place large serving plate on top of cake pan, centering cake. Invert cake. Shake slightly if necessary. Remove pan. Serve warm or at room temperature, with whipped cream or CRÈME FRAÎCHE if desired.

8 ounces frozen peach slices

1 cup dark brown sugar

1/2 cup butter

1/2 cup granulated sugar

1/2 cup molasses

2 cups all-purpose flour

1/2 teaspoon baking soda

1-1/2 teaspoons ground ginger

1/2 teaspoon cinnamon

1/2 cup buttermilk

Preheat oven to 350°

CRÈME FRAÎCHE is a wickedly wonderful dessert topping. You can make your own version of this delight by mixing 3 tablespoons of buttermilk with 1 cup heavy cream in a small jar. Chill 2 days, then shake until thickened. Use within a week in place of whipped cream.

POPPY SEED LEMON CAKE

10" Tube Cake

1/4 cup poppy seeds
1/4 cup buttermilk
4 eggs, separated
1 cup butter, softened
2 cups sugar
1 teaspoon lemon
  extract
1 teaspoon almond
  extract
2-1/2 cups cake flour
1 teaspoon baking
  soda
2 teaspoons baking
  powder
1 cup buttermilk
zest of two lemons

Preheat oven to 350°

The nuttiness of poppy seeds combined with the refreshing taste of lemon gives this cake a very distinctive flavor. Try toasting leftovers.

Grease and flour a 10" bundt or tube pan.

In a small bowl, soak poppy seeds in 1/4 cup buttermilk for 15 minutes.

Meanwhile, beat egg whites until soft peaks form. Set aside.

In a large mixing bowl, cream together butter and sugar. Mix in egg yolks, one at a time, beating well after each addition. Beat in extracts and poppy seeds.

Sift together flour, baking soda and baking powder. Add dry ingredients and buttermilk alternately to creamed mixture. Beat well.

Stir in a small amount of egg whites to lighten batter. Fold in remaining egg whites and lemon zest.

Pour into prepared pan. Bake 70 to 75 minutes until cake tests done. Cake will be a deep brown. Let sit 5 minutes. Turn out onto a wire rack to cool completely.

Glaze with LEMON ICING (See FRUIT ICINGS).

RUM RAISIN POUND CAKE

9" x 5" Loaf Cake

A dense, full-flavored cake. We imagine this would be Captain Hook's favorite.

Grease and flour a 9" x 5" loaf pan.

Soak raisins in rum, preferably overnight. Drain. Toss raisins in 2 tablespoons of the flour.

Cream together butter and sugar. Beat in eggs and vanilla. Sift together remaining flour, baking powder, baking soda, salt, and cinnamon. Beat dry ingredients, alternately with buttermilk, into creamed mixture. Stir in raisins and orange zest.

Bake about 70 minutes until cake tests done. Cool 10 minutes in pan on wire rack. Turn out on rack to cool completely.

Glaze with RUM ICING.

1 cup raisins
1/2 cup dark rum
2-1/4 cups all-purpose flour, divided
1-1/2 cups sugar
3/4 cup softened butter
3 eggs
1/2 teaspoon vanilla extract
1/2 teaspoon baking powder
1/4 teaspoon baking soda
1/4 teaspoon salt
1/2 teaspoon cinnamon
3/4 cup buttermilk
2 teaspoons grated orange zest

Preheat oven to 350°

TOASTED COCONUT LAYER CAKE

9" Two-layer Cake

1-1/4 cups flaked coconut

1/2 cup softened butter

1-1/2 cups sugar

3 eggs

1-1/2 teaspoons vanilla extract

2-1/4 cups all-purpose flour

1-1/2 teaspoons baking powder

1/2 teaspoon baking soda

1 teaspoon salt

1-1/4 cups buttermilk

Preheat oven to 375°

A light yellow cake subtly flavored with coconut.

Grease and flour two 9" cake pans.

Spread coconut on baking sheet. Bake about 5 minutes until well toasted. Check often, as coconut can burn easily. Set aside 1/2 cup to sprinkle on top of frosted cake.

In a large mixing bowl, cream together butter and sugar. Add eggs, one at a time, beating well after each addition. Stir in vanilla.

Sift together flour, baking powder, baking soda and salt. Add alternately, with buttermilk, to creamed mixture. Beat well. Stir in 3/4 cup toasted coconut.

Pour into prepared pans. Bake for 25 to 30 minutes until cake tests done. Cool in pan 10 minutes on wire rack. Turn cakes out and cool completely.

Frost with EASY MERINGUE FROSTING. Sprinkle top with reserved toasted coconut.

TRADITIONAL RED VELVET CAKE

9" Two-layer Cake

Originally known as Waldorf Astoria Cake, this traditional buttermilk cake had been ignored for several years. It is now making a comeback in gourmet food circles. Apparently, the novelty of its shocking, "Frankly Scarlet..." hue appeals to yet another generation.

Grease two 9" round cake pans well. Line bottoms with wax or parchment paper circles. Grease paper. Flour pans.

In large mixing bowl, cream together butter and sugar. Beat in eggs. Beat in food coloring, cocoa and salt.

Sift flour with baking soda and baking powder. Add dry ingredients to creamed mixture alternately with buttermilk and vanilla. Add vinegar. Beat well. Batter will be thin.

Divide batter evenly between prepared pans.

Bake 30 minutes until cake tests done. Let sit 5 minutes. Turn out on wire racks to cool, peeling off paper. Cool completely.

This cake is traditionally frosted with CREAM CHEESE FROSTING.

1/2 cup butter
1-1/2 cups sugar
2 eggs, beaten
2 ounces red food coloring
2 tablespoons cocoa
1 teaspoon salt
2-1/4 cups sifted cake flour
1 teaspoon baking soda
2 teaspoons baking powder
1 cup buttermilk
1 teaspoon vanilla extract
1 teaspoon white vinegar

Preheat oven to 350°

CARAMEL FROSTING

2 cups granulated
  sugar
1/2 cup softened
  butter
1 cup buttermilk
1 teaspoon baking
  soda
1 teaspoon vanilla
  extract
1 to 2 cups
  confectioners sugar
1/2 to 1 cup
  buttermilk

This cooked frosting gives a smooth, professional ganache finish. If you've never attempted a cooked frosting before, you've missed out on a lot of fun. The caramelization process is like magic.

In a large, heavy saucepan, over low heat, cook granulated sugar, butter, buttermilk and baking soda, stirring often until butter melts. Cease stirring and continue to cook until candy thermometer registers 236° and mixture comes to the soft ball stage. (Drop a very small amount of syrup into a glass of cold water. It should form a small ball that, when pressed between your thumb and forefinger, forms a flat, soft disc.) Remove from heat. Stir in vanilla.

Set the pan in a bowl of cold water. Beat the mixture until it starts to stiffen. Remove pan from cold water.

Add confectioners sugar and buttermilk. Beat to desired consistency, adding more confectioners sugar and/or buttermilk as necessary.

CREAM CHEESE FROSTING

Enough to fill & frost a 9" layer or 9"x 13" sheet cake

1 stick softened butter
8 ounces cream
  cheese, softened
1 pound sifted
  confectioners sugar
  (about 5 cups)

Cream together butter and cream cheese. Add sugar and mix until smooth.

CREAMY CHOCOLATE FROSTING

Enough to fill & frost a 9" layer or 9"x 13" sheet cake

In a double boiler, melt chocolate.

In a medium bowl, mix confectioners sugar, cream cheese, buttermilk and vanilla until smooth. Stir in chocolate.

5 ounces semi-sweet chocolate

2-1/2 cups sifted confectioners sugar

6 ounces cream cheese, softened

2 tablespoons buttermilk

1 teaspoon vanilla extract

EASY MERINGUE FROSTING

Enough to fill & frost a 9" layer or 9"x 13" sheet cake

In a small saucepan, over medium heat, bring sugar and water to a boil. Cook for 5 minutes.

Meanwhile, in a large mixing bowl, beat egg whites with salt to form soft peaks. Using an electric mixer, add hot sugar syrup in a slow, thin stream to egg whites, beating continuously. Beat in vanilla. Continue to beat until frosting is thick enough to spread.

1 cup granulated sugar

1/2 cup water

2 egg whites

pinch of salt

1 teaspoon vanilla extract

FRUIT ICINGS

About 1 cup

These simple icings are perfect for pound cakes, cookies and muffins.

In a medium bowl, mix confectioners sugar and fruit juice until smooth.

2 cups sifted confectioners sugar

1/4 cup lemon, orange, grapefruit, strawberry or any strained fruit juice

RUM ICING

About 1/2 cup

1 cup confectioners
  sugar

1/2 teaspoon rum
  extract

3 to 4 teaspoons water

In a medium bowl, mix confectioners sugar, extract and one teaspoon of water at a time until smooth.

SHEET CAKE CHOCOLATE FROSTING

Enough to frost a 9" x 13" sheet cake

3 ounces (3 squares)
  unsweetened
  chocolate

2 cups confectioners
  sugar, sifted

1/2 cup butter

2 teaspoons vanilla
  extract

Oftentimes, a full frosting recipe is too much for a sheet cake. This small batch is just right for EVERYDAY CHOCOLATE CAKE.

In a double boiler, melt chocolate.

In the meantime, cream sugar and butter. Add chocolate and vanilla. Beat until smooth.

Quick Breads &
Coffee Cakes

BACON MUENSTER SODA BREAD

9" Round Loaf

This bread is full-flavored, with a rustic crust and a popover-like taste.

Grease a 9" round cake pan.

In a large bowl, combine flour, salt, baking soda and sugar. Stir in bacon and cheese to coat and separate.

Stir in buttermilk just until ingredients are moistened.

Turn dough out onto lightly floured surface. Knead 8 to 10 turns. Shape into a round loaf and place in prepared pan.

Bake 75 minutes until well browned. Remove from pan and place on wire rack to cool slightly. Serve warm.

4 cups all-purpose flour

1 teaspoon salt

1/2 tablespoon baking soda

1 tablespoon sugar

5 slices crisp cooked bacon, crumbled

1 cup (2 to 3 ounces) shredded muenster cheese

2 cups buttermilk

Preheat oven to 350°

BANANA BREAD

One 9"x 5" Loaf

1/2 cup butter

1-1/3 cups sugar

2 eggs, well beaten

1/2 cup buttermilk

1 teaspoon vanilla
extract

1 cup (two medium)
mashed ripe
bananas

2 cups all-purpose
flour

1 teaspoon baking
powder

1 teaspoon baking
soda

1 teaspoon salt

1/2 cup chopped
walnuts

Preheat over to 375°

A moist, delicious version of this old favorite.

Grease and flour a 9" x 5" loaf pan.

In a large bowl, cream together butter and sugar. Add eggs, buttermilk, vanilla and bananas. Mix well.

Sift together flour, baking powder, baking soda, and salt. Combine with wet ingredients. Stir in nuts.

Pour into prepared pan. Bake about 50 minutes until bread tests done. Remove from pan and cool on wire rack.

> If your bananas are ripe but you're not ready to use them, pop them unpeeled into the freezer. The skins will blacken but the flesh will be fine for that next banana recipe.

PUMPKIN CORNBREAD

8" Square Bread

This is perfect for Thanksgiving.

Grease an 8" square baking pan.

Stir flour, cornmeal, baking powder, baking soda, brown sugar, salt and ginger together until well mixed. Mix eggs, butter, buttermilk and pumpkin. Stir into dry ingredients just to moisten.

Pour into prepared pan. Bake 35 to 40 minutes until bread tests done.

You can also bake these as muffins, filling greased or paper-lined cups about 2/3 full and reducing baking time by 5 to 10 minutes.

Serve hot with HONEY BUTTER.

1-1/4 cups all-purpose flour

3/4 cup cornmeal

2 teaspoons baking powder

3/4 teaspoon baking soda

1/3 cup dark brown sugar

1/2 teaspoon salt

3/4 teaspoon ground ginger

2 eggs, beaten

1/4 cup melted butter

2/3 cup buttermilk

3/4 cup pumpkin or squash puree

Preheat oven to 350°

PUMPKIN PRUNE HAZELNUT BREAD

Two 9"x 5" Loaves

3-1/3 cups all-purpose flour

2 teaspoons baking soda

1/2 teaspoon baking powder

1-1/2 teaspoons salt

1 teaspoon cinnamon

1/2 teaspoon freshly grated nutmeg

1/2 teaspoon ground cloves

2/3 cup softened butter

2 cups pumpkin puree

4 beaten eggs

2-1/2 cups sugar

2/3 cup buttermilk

1 cup chopped pitted prunes, dusted with flour

1 cup chopped hazelnuts

Grease and flour two 9" x 5" loaf pans.

Sift together flour, baking soda, baking powder, salt, cinnamon, nutmeg and cloves. Set aside.

In a large mixing bowl, mix together butter, pumpkin, eggs, sugar and buttermilk. Add dry ingredients. Mix just until blended. Fold in prunes and nuts.

Pour into prepared pans. Bake for 1 hour or until breads test done.

Cool on wire rack 15 minutes. Turn out and cool completely.

Preheat oven to 350°

RASPBERRY JAM BREAD

Two 9"x 5" Loaves

This very moist tea bread is redolent of the raspberry patch.

Grease two 9" x 5" loaf pans well.

Sift togcthcr flour, salt, baking soda, baking powder, cinnamon, nutmeg and allspice. Stir in lemon zest.

Cream sugar and butter well. Beat in eggs and vanilla. Stir in jam. Beat in dry ingredients alternately with buttermilk. Stir in walnuts.

Pour into prepared pans. Bake 75 to 85 minutes until breads test done. Cool on wire rack 15 minutes. Turn out and cool completely.

3 cups all-purpose flour

1-1/2 teaspoons salt

1 teaspoon baking soda

1 teaspoon baking powder

1 teaspoon cinnamon

1/2 teaspoon freshly grated nutmeg

1/2 teaspoon ground allspice

2 teaspoons grated lemon zest

1-1/2 cups sugar

3/4 cup softened butter

4 eggs

1 teaspoon vanilla extract

18-ounce jar raspberry jam

1 cup buttermilk

1 cup chopped walnuts or pecans

Preheat oven to 325°

ROADHOUSE LOAF

One 9"x 5" Loaf

1/2 cup Grape-Nuts®
cereal

1 cup buttermilk

3/4 cup sugar

1 egg, beaten

2 tablespoons melted
butter

2 cups all-purpose
flour

1 teaspoon baking
powder

1/2 teaspoon baking
soda

1/2 teaspoon salt

1 teaspoon cinnamon

Preheat oven to 375°

Pudding made from Grape-Nuts® cereal is standard fare in diners all over the northeast. This loaf is like having your pudding by the slice.

Grease and flour a 9" x 5" loaf pan.

Mix cereal and buttermilk. Let sit about 30 minutes.

Stir in sugar, egg and butter until well combined. Sift flour with baking powder, baking soda, salt and cinnamon. Stir into cereal mixture until completely combined. Dough will be heavy and thick.

Turn into prepared pan. Bake 35 to 40 minutes until browned and center tests done. Cool in pan a few minutes before turning out on a rack to cool completely.

RUTH KELLY'S IRISH SODA BREAD

8" Round Loaf

Dedicated to Susan's mom, who always makes sure there is plenty of love and lots to eat.

Grease an 8" or 9" round cake pan.

In a large mixing bowl, combine flour, baking powder, baking soda, salt, raisins, caraway seeds and sugar. Mix well. Stir in buttermilk, just to moisten.

Turn dough out on a lightly floured surface. Knead for one minute. Shape into a ball. Set in prepared pan. A cross cut on the top with a sharp knife makes a nice appearance.

Bake about 45 to 50 minutes until golden brown and crisp.

2 cups all-purpose flour (or use up to 1/2 cup whole wheat flour)

1-1/2 teaspoons baking powder

1/2 teaspoon baking soda

1 teaspoon salt

1 cup raisins (optional)

1 tablespoon caraway seeds (optional)

1/4 cup sugar (optional)

1 cup buttermilk

Preheat oven to 350°

STEAMED NEW ENGLAND BROWN BREAD

1 Loaf

2/3 cup all-purpose
  flour
2/3 cup whole wheat
  flour
2/3 cup cornmeal
1 teaspoon salt
3/4 teaspoon baking
  soda
1/2 cup molasses
1 cup buttermilk
3/4 cup raisins

An unusual but very traditional way of making bread. It's impressive, easy and a natural accompaniment to Boston baked beans.

Butter a 13-ounce or larger coffee can with one end removed.

Place a deep pan, taller than the coffee can, on stove burner. Place a rack, trivet or small balls of aluminum foil in the bottom of the pan.

Mix flours, cornmeal, salt and baking soda. Stir in molasses and buttermilk until mixture is well combined. Fold in raisins.

Pour into prepared can. Cover top tightly with aluminum foil. Set can on rack in pan. Add hot water to reach halfway up can. Cover pan tightly. Bring to boil. Reduce heat to a simmer and steam bread about 2-1/2 hours. Do not uncover.

Remove can from pan and invert on wire rack. Cool 10 minutes. Remove remaining end of can and slide bread out. Serve warm with cream cheese.

SUPPER HOE CAKES

6 to 8 Cakes

Serve these pioneer-inspired cakes with stews or soups.

Mix cornmeal, flour, salt, sugar and baking soda well. Stir in butter and buttermilk. Stir in raisins if using.

Heat lightly greased skillet over medium heat until hot. Drop batter by slightly heaping 1/4 cupfuls into skillet. Do not spread batter. Cook until dry and beginning to brown around bottom edges. Turn and brown other side.

Serve hot with butter.

1 cup cornmeal
1/2 cup all-purpose
  flour
1/2 teaspoon salt
1 tablespoon sugar
1 teaspoon baking
  soda
1 tablespoon melted
  butter
1 cup buttermilk
1/2 cup raisins
  (optional)

SUN-DRIED TOMATO BREAD

One 9"x 5" Loaf

2-1/2 cups all-purpose
flour

2 teaspoons baking
powder

1 teaspoon salt

1/2 teaspoon baking
soda

1/3 cup chopped, oil-
packed sun-dried
tomatoes, drained
(reserve 2
tablespoons oil)

1 bunch scallions,
thinly sliced

6 ounces chopped
provolone cheese

1 teaspoon dried
oregano

1/2 teaspoon freshly
ground black pepper

1/3 cup toasted
walnuts

2 tablespoons softened
butter

2 tablespoons sugar

2 cloves roasted
garlic, mashed

2 eggs

1-1/4 cups buttermilk

Preheat oven to 350°

*A sophisticated quick bread. We imagine it
was this type of flavor that inspired,
"A jug of wine, a loaf of bread and thou..."*

Grease and flour a 9" x 5" loaf pan.

In a large mixing bowl, sift together flour,
baking powder, salt and baking soda. Add
tomatoes, scallions, provolone, oregano,
pepper and nuts.

In a small bowl, mix reserved oil, butter and
sugar until smooth. Add garlic, eggs and
buttermilk. Mix well.

Combine dry and wet ingredients just to
moisten.

Pour into prepared pan.

Bake 40 to 45 minutes or until bread tests
done. Cool in pan for 5 minutes. Turn out
onto a wire rack to cool slightly. Serve warm.

Sun-dried tomatoes bring an incredibly
concentrated tomato flavor to your
creations. We prefer the satiny texture of
the tomatoes packed in real olive oil.
Plain sun-dried tomatoes can be
reconstituted in hot water.

SOUTHERN MAMA'S MOIST CORNBREAD

9"x 13" Bread

You'll never buy another box of cornbread mix again!

Grease and flour a 9" x 13" baking pan.

In a large bowl, stir together cornmeal, flour, sugar, baking powder, baking soda and salt until well mixed. Add eggs, buttermilk and butter. Stir just until ingredients are moistened. Batter will be lumpy.

Spread evenly in prepared pan.

Bake 40 to 45 minutes until golden brown and tests done.

2 cups cornmeal

2 cups all-purpose flour

1/2 cup sugar

1 tablespoon plus 1 teaspoon baking powder

1 teaspoon baking soda

1 teaspoon salt

3 beaten eggs

2 cups buttermilk

6 tablespoons melted butter, cooled

Preheat oven to 350°

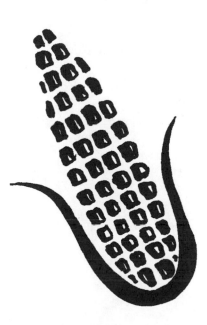

ANNA'S APPLE COFFEE CAKE

9" Square Cake

Topping:

1/3 cup dark brown sugar

1 teaspoon cinnamon

1/3 cup chopped walnuts

Cake:

1/4 cup softened butter

2/3 cup dark brown sugar

1 egg

1-1/2 cups buttermilk

1 teaspoon vanilla extract

1/2 teaspoon cinnamon

1/2 teaspoon ground cloves

1/2 teaspoon salt

2 cups all-purpose flour

1 teaspoon baking powder

1 teaspoon baking soda

2 large chopped apples, about 2 cups

1/2 cup raisins or dried cranberries

Preheat oven to 350°

A never-fail, no-fuss, moist coffee cake.

Topping:

In a small bowl, mix together brown sugar and cinnamon. Stir in nuts. Set aside.

Cake:

Grease and flour a 9" square baking pan.

In a large mixing bowl, cream together butter and sugar. Beat in egg, buttermilk, vanilla, cinnamon, cloves and salt.

Sift together flour, baking powder and baking soda. Stir into butter mixture to make a smooth batter. Stir in apples and raisins.

Pour batter into prepared pan. Sprinkle evenly with topping.

Bake 40 to 45 minutes until cake tests done. Cool slightly before cutting.

> For baking, Granny Smith and Empire apples are the most reliable for taste and texture.

FIG CAKE

9" x 13" Coffee Cake

This giant version of "Mr. Newton's" cookie makes a vitamin-packed breakfast treat.

Grease and flour a 9" x 13" baking pan.

In a large mixing bowl, cream together sugar and oil. Beat in eggs. Sift together flour, salt, baking soda, nutmeg and cinnamon. Add dry ingredients to creamed mixture alternately with buttermilk. Stir in figs and pecans.

Bake 55 to 65 minutes until cake tests done.

Glaze with a FRUIT ICING if desired.

2 cups sugar
1 cup vegetable oil
3 eggs
2 cups all-purpose
  flour
1 teaspoon salt
1 teaspoon baking
  soda
1/2 teaspoon nutmeg
1 teaspoon cinnamon
2/3 cup buttermilk
1 cup chopped figs
2 cups pecans, toasted

Preheat oven to 350°

GLAZED BING CHERRY COFFEE CAKE

9" Square Cake

Cake:

1/2 cup butter

1-1/2 cups sugar

2 eggs

1/4 cup buttermilk

1 teaspoon vanilla
extract

1/2 teaspoon baking
soda

1 teaspoon baking
powder

1 teaspoon salt

2 cups all-purpose
flour

1/2 teaspoon ground
cardamom
(optional)

12 ounces frozen
sweet cherries

Glaze:

1 cup confectioners
sugar

1/2 teaspoon almond
extract

1 tablespoon water

Preheat oven to 350°

Frozen cherries make this a year-round favorite.

Grease and flour a 9" square cake pan.

Cake:

In a large mixing bowl, cream together butter and sugar. Beat in eggs. Stir in buttermilk and vanilla.

Sift together baking soda, baking powder, salt, flour and cardamom. Mix wet and dry ingredients together. Stir in cherries.

Pour batter into prepared pan. Bake 50 to 60 minutes until cake tests done. Cool 5 minutes. Turn out onto wire rack to cool. Invert onto serving plate. Apply glaze.

Glaze:

In a small bowl, mix together confectioners sugar, extract and water, adding more water in drops if necessary.

LEMON CURD COFFEE CAKE with LEMON GLAZE

9"x 13" Coffee Cake

Oh, the English. They are so civilized.

Lemon curd:

In a medium heavy saucepan, whisk together sugar, lemon juice and egg yolks. Over moderate heat, whisking constantly, cook mixture (do not allow to boil) about 15 minutes or until candy thermometer registers 175° and curd has the consistency of cooled pudding. Set aside.

Cake:

Grease and flour a 9" x 13" baking pan.

Cream butter and sugar. Beat in eggs one at a time. Add lemon zest. Sift flour with baking powder and baking soda. Add dry ingredients to creamed mixture alternately with buttermilk and vanilla. Spread half of batter in prepared pan. Carefully spread with all of lemon curd, leaving 1" border. Sprinkle with half of pecans. Dollop remaining batter over lemon curd and spread carefully to cover lemon curd. Sprinkle with remaining pecans. Bake 35 to 40 minutes until cake is firm to the touch. Place on wire rack and cool in pan.

Glaze:

Mix confectioners sugar and lemon juice to make thin glaze. Drizzle over cooled cake.

Lemon Curd:
3/4 cup sugar
1/2 cup fresh lemon juice
6 egg yolks

Cake:
1 cup butter
2 cups sugar
4 eggs
grated zest of 1 lemon
3 cups all-purpose flour
1-1/2 teaspoons baking powder
1/2 teaspoon baking soda
1 cup buttermilk
1 teaspoon vanilla extract
1 cup broken pecans (optional)

Glaze:
3/4 cup confectioners sugar
1-1/2 tablespoons lemon juice

Preheat oven to 350°

PISTACHIO SEMOLINA CAKE with VANILLA SYRUP

Two 9" Round Cakes

Cake:

1/2 cup softened
  butter

1 cup sugar

1 cup semolina flour

3/4 cup all-purpose
  flour

1 teaspoon baking
  powder

1/2 teaspoon baking
  soda

1/4 teaspoon salt

2 eggs + 1 egg yolk

2/3 cup buttermilk

3/4 cup natural,
  unsalted, shelled
  pistachio nuts

Syrup:

3/4 cup sugar

3/4 cup water

1 teaspoon lemon
  juice

1 teaspoon vanilla
  extract

cinnamon stick
  (optional)

Preheat oven to 350°

This cake is simply delicious. If you don't have pistachio nuts, it's fine to omit them.

Cake:

Grease and flour two 9" round cake pans.

In a large mixing bowl, cream together butter and sugar. Add flours, baking powder, baking soda, salt, eggs and egg yolk. Mix well. Stir in buttermilk. Fold in nuts.

Pour into prepared pans.

Bake 40 minutes until cake tests done.

Syrup:

Meanwhile, make the syrup.

In a heavy saucepan, simmer sugar, water and lemon juice about 10 minutes until sugar is completely dissolved. Remove from heat. Stir in vanilla and cool 30 minutes.

Assembly:

Cool cakes in pans 10 minutes on a wire rack. Poke holes all over top of cakes with a toothpick. Drizzle each cake with half of the syrup.

Cool in pans. Turn out.

> Substitute cornmeal for the semolina flour for a different flavor and heartier texture.

PRETTY PEARS ALL IN A ROW COFFEE CAKE

9"x 13" Coffee Cake

Patisserie pretty!

Grease and flour a 9" x 13" baking pan.

Halve the pears. Peel and core. Slice thinly, keeping the slices together in their pear form. Set aside.

In a large mixing bowl, cream together butter, sugar and almond paste. Mix in egg and extract. Sift together flour, baking powder, baking soda and salt. Add dry ingredients to creamed mixture alternately with buttermilk. Spread evenly in prepared pan.

Slide sliced pear halves on top of batter in two rows. (Don't press.) Brush pears with warm honey and sprinkle sugar on uncovered batter.

Bake about 50 minutes until cake tests done.

Cool in pan on a wire rack.

2 large firm, ripe pears
1/2 cup softened butter
1 cup sugar
1/4 cup almond paste
1 beaten egg
1 teaspoon vanilla extract
2-1/2 cups all-purpose flour
2 teaspoons baking powder
1 teaspoon baking soda
1/2 teaspoon salt
1 cup buttermilk
1/4 cup warmed honey
additional sugar for sprinkling

Preheat oven to 350°

SUGAR PLUM COFFEE CAKE

9"x 13" Cake

Topping:
3/4 cup dark brown
  sugar
3 tablespoons all-
  purpose flour
2 teaspoons cinnamon
1/2 teaspoon salt
3 tablespoons softened
  butter

Cake:
16 Italian blue plums,
  pitted and halved
1/4 cup sugar
2 cups all-purpose
  flour
1/2 teaspoon salt
1/2 teaspoon baking
  soda
3/4 cup sugar
1/4 cup softened
  butter
1 egg, well beaten
1/2 cup buttermilk

*Your sugar plum fairies will love this rich,
slightly sticky cake. Begin your day with a
sweet start or serve this cake for dessert.*

Topping:

Mix brown sugar, flour, cinnamon, salt and
butter until well combined and crumbly. Set
aside.

Cake:

Grease and flour a 9" x 13" baking pan.

Toss plum halves with 1/4 cup sugar until
well coated. Set aside.

Sift flour, salt, baking soda and sugar into
mixing bowl. Cut in butter to make coarse
crumbs. Mix egg with buttermilk. Stir into
dry ingredients just to moisten.

Spread half of batter in prepared pan. Cover
with half of plums. Sprinkle with half of
topping mixture. Repeat layers.

Bake 50 to 60 minutes until cake tests done.
Serve warm, at room temperature or reheated.
Cover leftovers to maintain freshness.

Preheat oven to 350°

Muffins & Doughnuts

Mmmmmm......MUFFINS

Commercially prepared muffins are tasteless, overpriced and packed with preservatives. At what price "convenience," when homemade muffins are so good and so easy to prepare?

Since muffins should, literally, be tossed together (too much mixing ruins the texture), they are one of the simplest "little cakes" to make. We like to have several different kinds in the freezer to assemble baskets of assorted muffins for special breakfasts and brunches.

Muffins are delicious for everyday breakfasts, served straight out of the oven or popped, frozen, into the microwave (25 seconds) or toaster oven (5 minutes at 350°). If you haven't time to eat them at the table, you can eat them on the run.

They freeze very well and travel easily. Stuff them in lunch boxes for schoolday desserts or inexpensive coffee breaks.

Making muffins:

✓ Prepare the wet and dry ingredients separately, making sure the dry ingredients are well mixed and the wet ingredients are well blended.

✓ Combine the wet and dry ingredients just until the dry ingredients are moistened.

✓ Fill muffin cups to nearly full.

✓ For virtually no clean up, fill foil muffin cups with batter and set them directly on a baking sheet.

✓ If you use paper muffin cup liners, spray them lightly with a non-stick vegetable spray.

✓ If you bake the batter directly in muffin pans, grease the cups well. If you've greased all the cups but don't fill them all, then you should fill the unused cups with water. There's no need to fill ungreased cups with water.

✓ We used standard-size muffin pans. Adjust baking times for other size pans.

✓ Muffins are done when their tops are golden and a toothpick inserted in their centers comes out with no moist crumbs clinging to it.

BASIC MUFFIN BATTER

12 to 18 Muffins

No more heavy, dry muffins. Buttermilk muffins bake up light and moist every time.

See BASIC MUFFIN ADDITIONS for muffin variations.

Grease muffin cups or line with paper.

Sift flour with baking powder, baking soda and salt. Stir in sugar.

In a separate bowl, mix buttermilk, eggs, butter and vanilla.

Stir into dry ingredients just to moisten. Spoon batter into muffin cups.

Bake about 20 minutes, until muffins test done. Transfer to wire rack to cool slightly. Serve warm.

2 cups all-purpose flour

1 tablespoon baking powder

1/2 teaspoon baking soda

1 teaspoon salt

1/4 cup sugar

1 cup buttermilk

2 eggs, beaten

1/2 cup butter, melted and cooled

1 teaspoon vanilla extract

Preheat oven to 400°

Basic Muffin Additions

BLUEBERRY MUFFINS:

After stirring in dry ingredients, fold in 1 cup fresh blueberries or unthawed frozen blueberries.

STRAWBERRY BANANA MUFFINS:

Add an additional 1/4 cup sugar to BASIC MUFFIN BATTER. After mixing batter, fold in 1/2 cup chopped walnuts, 1 small diced banana and 2 cups coarsely chopped, fresh or unthawed frozen strawberries.

CHERRY MUFFINS:

Substitute almond extract for vanilla. After stirring in dry ingredients, fold in 1 cup fresh pitted or unthawed frozen sweet cherries.

RASPBERRY LEMON MUFFINS:

Add grated zest of 1/2 lemon to dry ingredients. After stirring in dry ingredients, fold in 1 cup fresh raspberries or thawed, well-drained frozen raspberries.

JELLY DOUGHNUT MUFFINS:

Prepare BASIC MUFFIN BATTER. Fill muffin cups about 1/3 full. Add a heaping teaspoon of favorite jelly or preserves. Cover with remaining batter.

FIG OR DATE MUFFINS:

Add 1/2 teaspoon ground cardamom to dry ingredients. After stirring in dry ingredients, fold in 1 cup chopped dried figs or dates.

BANANA PECAN MUFFINS

12 to 16 Muffins

1/2 cup butter

1 cup sugar

2 eggs, beaten

2 large ripe bananas, mashed

1/2 cup pecans, chopped

1 teaspoon vanilla extract

2 cups all-purpose flour

1 teaspoon salt

1 teaspoon baking powder

1/2 teaspoon baking soda

1 cup buttermilk

Preheat oven to 400°

These are the best banana muffins you'll ever make. The natural sugar in the bananas yields a caramelized top.

Grease muffin cups or line with paper.

In a large mixing bowl, cream together butter and sugar. Beat in eggs, one at a time. Stir in bananas, pecans and vanilla.

In a separate bowl, combine flour, salt, baking powder and baking soda.

Add dry ingredients alternately with buttermilk to creamed mixture. Mix just to moisten.

Spoon batter into muffin cups. Bake until lightly golden and muffins test done, 15 to 18 minutes. Transfer to wire rack to cool slightly. Serve warm.

BOUNCEBERRY MUFFINS

12 Muffins

Known to the Pilgrims as bounceberries, cranberries add a hint of tartness to these beautiful harvest-colored corn muffins.

Grease muffin cups or line with paper.

In a large mixing bowl, combine cornmeal, flour, salt, baking powder and baking soda.

Stir in maple syrup, eggs, butter and buttermilk. Mix, just to moisten. Stir in cranberries.

Spoon batter into muffin cups. Bake until lightly golden and muffins test done, 15 to 18 minutes. Transfer to wire rack to cool slightly. Serve warm.

1 cup cornmeal

1 cup all-purpose flour

1/2 teaspoon salt

1 teaspoon baking powder

1/2 teaspoon baking soda

1/2 cup maple syrup

2 eggs

4 tablespoons melted butter

1/2 cup buttermilk

1/2 cup chopped fresh or frozen cranberries

Preheat oven to 375°

MAPLE RAISIN GINGER MUFFINS

3 Dozen Small Muffins

1 cup butter or
vegetable shortening

1 cup sugar

3 eggs

1 cup real maple
syrup

1 cup buttermilk

3 cups all-purpose
flour

1-3/4 teaspoons
baking soda

2 teaspoons ground
ginger

2 teaspoons cinnamon

1 teaspoon freshly
grated nutmeg

1/2 teaspoon salt

1 cup raisins

Preheat oven to 375°

Light, mildly spiced little tea cakes.

Grease muffin cups or line with paper.

Cream butter and sugar. Beat in eggs one at a time. Beat in maple syrup and buttermilk.

Sift flour with baking soda, ginger, cinnamon, nutmeg and salt. Stir in raisins, coating well with the flour mixture. Stir dry ingredients into creamed mixture just to mix.

Spoon batter into muffin cups. Bake about 15 minutes until muffins test done. Transfer to wire rack to cool slightly. Serve warm.

RICH APPLE PIE MUFFINS

These are rich, but not overly sweet, muffins.

Grease muffin cups or line with paper.

Peel apples and cut in 1/4" or smaller dice to make about 1-1/2 cups. Set aside.

Sift flour with sugar, salt, baking powder, cinnamon and nutmeg. Add apples and toss to coat. Stir in butter. Add egg, buttermilk and vanilla. Mix just until moistened. Batter will be very thick.

Spoon batter into muffin cups. Bake about 15 minutes until golden brown and muffins test done. Transfer to wire rack to cool slightly. Serve warm.

2 medium tart apples

3 cups all-purpose flour

1 cup dark brown sugar

1 teaspoon salt

4-1/2 teaspoons baking powder

1 tablespoon cinnamon

1/8 teaspoon freshly grated nutmeg

1 cup butter, melted

1 egg

1 cup buttermilk

1/2 teaspoon vanilla extract

Preheat oven to 375°

BUTTERMILK CAKE DOUGHNUTS

2 Dozen

3 cups all-purpose
  flour

1 cup cake flour

1 teaspoon salt

1 teaspoon baking
  soda

1 teaspoon baking
  powder

1 teaspoon freshly
  grated nutmeg

2 eggs

1 cup sugar

1/2 cup melted
  vegetable
  shortening, cooled to
  lukewarm

1 cup buttermilk

vegetable oil for deep-
  frying

1 cup sugar mixed
  with 1 teaspoon
  cinnamon

Sift together flours, salt, baking soda, baking powder and nutmeg. Set aside.

In a large mixing bowl, beat together eggs and sugar. Add shortening and buttermilk. Stir in dry ingredients.

On a dry, well-floured surface, knead lightly until dough is not sticky. Dough will be soft. Divide dough in half. Pat dough out 1/4" thick. Cut with doughnut cutter.

In deep oil, fry doughnuts until well browned on both sides, turning once. The holes should turn themselves.

Drain on absorbent paper. Cool slightly. Toss in sugar/cinnamon mixture.

Heat oil to 375°

RAISED DOUGHNUTS

2 Dozen

We originally earmarked this recipe for a chapter to be entitled "Things to Do Just Once" but, like most other "Oh, I just couldn't...but did anyway" experiences, yeast doughnuts are truly memorable.

In a large mixing bowl, combine water, yeast, buttermilk, salt and 2 cups of the flour. Cover and let rise 30 minutes.

Melt butter and shortening. Add to risen dough, with sugar, eggs and nutmeg. Add 1-1/2 cups of flour. Let rise again until light, about 45 minutes. Punch down.

Turn dough out onto a floured surface. Knead in additional flour if dough is too soft to handle. Divide dough into 2 parts. Cover each and let rest for 10 minutes.

Roll 1/2" thick. Cut with doughnut cutter. Arrange uncovered on a floured surface and let rise about 1 hour.

Fry doughnuts until browned on both sides, turning once. Drain on absorbent paper. Cool slightly. Toss in a mixture of 1 cup sugar and 1 teaspoon cinnamon, or confectioners sugar.

1/4 cup warm water
1 packet active dry yeast
1 cup lukewarm buttermilk
1 teaspoon salt
3-1/2 cups all-purpose flour, divided
3 tablespoons butter
2 tablespoons vegetable shortening
1 cup sugar
2 eggs, well beaten
1/2 teaspoon freshly grated nutmeg
vegetable oil for deep-frying

Heat oil to 375°

Scones

ABOUT SCONES

Although scones are one of the world's oldest forms of quick breads, many American cooks are unfamiliar with these wonderful creations and think them too exotic to try at home. Originally scones were griddle-fried, rustic breads, but through the ages they have evolved into sweet or savory, melt-in-your-mouth, oven-baked, shaggy textured biscuits.

Since scones share so many biscuit characteristics, please refer to the biscuit chapter for techniques and hints. Keep in mind, however, that scones are best made with all-purpose flour.

Scones freeze well. Reheat frozen scones in a 350° oven until heated through.

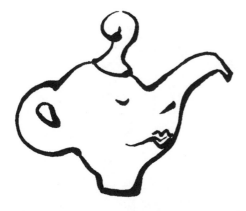

CHERRY ALMOND SCONES

1 Dozen Scones

You must make these. They're delicious!

In a large mixing bowl, combine flour, sugar, baking powder, baking soda and salt. Cut in butter until mixture resembles coarse meal. Stir in cherries and almonds.

In a small bowl, beat together egg and extract. Add egg mixture with buttermilk to dry ingredients. Stir with a fork to make a soft dough. Do not over mix.

Turn dough onto a lightly-floured surface. Knead 8 to 10 times. Divide dough into 2 equal parts. Pat each part into a 6" circle.

Place on a greased baking sheet. Brush tops with buttermilk. Sprinkle with sugar. Score each top, about halfway through, into 6 pie-shaped wedges.

Bake 15 to 17 minutes until golden brown.

Cut apart along score lines.

2 cups all-purpose flour
3 tablespoons sugar
2-1/2 teaspoons baking powder
1/2 teaspoon baking soda
1 teaspoon salt
1/4 cup chilled butter
1 cup dried cherries
1/3 cup toasted slivered almonds
1 egg, beaten
1/2 teaspoon almond extract
2/3 cup buttermilk
buttermilk for brushing tops
sugar for sprinkling tops

Preheat oven to 425°

SUSAN'S CRANBERRY LEMON SCONES

8 Scones

2 cups all-purpose
flour

1/4 cup sugar

2 teaspoons baking
powder

1/2 teaspoon salt

6 tablespoons chilled
butter

1/2 cup dried
cranberries

2 teaspoons grated
lemon zest

2/3 cup buttermilk

buttermilk for
brushing tops

1 teaspoon sugar

Preheat over to 425°

*This was Susan's first buttermilk scone
creation. It's still her favorite.*

In a large bowl, combine flour, 1/4 cup sugar,
baking powder and salt. Cut in butter until
mixture resembles coarse meal. Stir in
cranberries and lemon zest. Stir in buttermilk
with a fork until the dough holds together.

Gather dough into a ball and gently knead a
few times on a floured surface until smooth.
Pat out dough to an 8" circle. Cut circle into 8
wedges.

Place 2" apart on a greased baking sheet.
Brush tops with buttermilk. Sprinkle with
sugar.

Bake 15 to 20 minutes until lightly golden.

OATMEAL SCONES

These have a fine texture. Serve them as a special treat on a blustery morning.

In a medium-size bowl, combine oats and buttermilk. Let sit for 15 minutes.

In a large mixing bowl, combine flour, sugar, baking powder, salt and baking soda. Cut in butter until mixture resembles coarse meal.

Add oat-buttermilk mixture and egg to dry ingredients. Mix to moisten. Do not over mix.

Turn dough onto a lightly floured surface. Knead 5 times. Pat to form a circle 3/4" thick. Cut into 8 wedges. Separate and place on a greased baking sheet. Brush with maple syrup.

Bake 15 to 18 minutes until lightly golden.

1 cup quick-cooking oats

3/4 cup buttermilk

1 cup all-purpose flour

2 tablespoons dark brown sugar

1-1/2 teaspoons baking powder

1/2 teaspoon salt

1/2 teaspoon baking soda

4 tablespoons chilled butter

1 egg, beaten

real maple syrup for glazing

Preheat over to 425°

ORANGE PRUNE DROP SCONES

10 to 12 Scones

2-1/4 cups all-purpose
  flour
1/2 cup sugar
3 teaspoons baking
  powder
1/2 teaspoon salt
4 teaspoons orange
  zest
1/4 cup chilled butter
1 egg, beaten
1 to 1-1/4 cups
  buttermilk
1-1/2 cups chopped
  pitted prunes
sugar for sprinkling

Prunes have a public relations problem. This recipe gives them a well-deserved second chance.

In a large mixing bowl, combine flour, sugar, baking powder, salt and orange zest. Cut in butter until mixture resembles coarse meal.

Add egg and enough buttermilk to form a moist dough. Stir in prunes. Do not over mix.

Drop by 1/4 cupfuls on greased baking sheet. Sprinkle with sugar.

Bake 20 minutes until edges are lightly browned.

Preheat oven to 375°

PEANUT BUTTER and JAM SCONES

6 to 8 Large Scones

Warm, delicious memories of childhood.

Grease a 9" round cake pan and set aside.

Mix flour, sugar, baking powder, baking soda and salt. Cut in peanut butter until mixture resembles coarse meal.

Stir in egg and buttermilk to make a fairly firm dough. Turn out onto a lightly floured surface. Knead 5 times.

Divide dough into two parts, making one part slightly larger. Pat larger portion into prepared cake pan, pushing sides slightly up rim.

Spread jam thinly in center, leaving 1" border all around. Add more jam if needed, but keep jam layer thin. Pat remaining dough out to 8" circle and fit on top of jam. Bring edges of bottom dough layer up and seal to top layer.

Score top of dough in 6 to 8 wedges without cutting all the way through.

Bake about 25 minutes until golden brown. Let rest 10 minutes before cutting along score lines.

2 cups all-purpose flour
4 tablespoons sugar
3 teaspoons baking powder
3/4 teaspoon baking soda
1/2 teaspoon salt
1/4 cup crunchy peanut butter
1 egg, beaten
2/3 cup buttermilk
about 1/3 cup thick strawberry jam

Preheat oven to 425°

PUMPKIN WALNUT SCONES

8 Scones

1/4 cup sugar

1/2 teaspoon
cinnamon

1/4 teaspoon ground
ginger

1/4 teaspoon freshly
grated nutmeg

2-1/2 cups all-purpose
flour

3 teaspoons baking
powder

1/2 teaspoon baking
soda

1/4 teaspoon salt

8 tablespoons cold
butter, diced

1 cup pumpkin puree

1/4 cup buttermilk

1 cup currants

1/2 cup walnuts,
ground finely

buttermilk for
brushing tops

Preheat over to 400°

Trick or treat?

In a large bowl, combine sugar, cinnamon, ginger, nutmeg, flour, baking powder, baking soda and salt.

Cut in butter until mixture resembles coarse meal.

Add pumpkin and buttermilk. Mix until just moistened. Add currants and walnuts.

Gather dough into a ball and gently knead a few times on a floured surface until smooth. Pat out dough to a 9" circle. Cut circle into 8 wedges.

Place wedges 2" apart on a greased baking sheet and brush tops with buttermilk.

Bake 20 to 25 minutes until lightly golden.

WALNUT DATE DROP SCONES

Dates give these scones a grown-up sweetness that can't be beat.

In a large mixing bowl, combine flour, bran, baking powder, baking soda, salt, cinnamon and brown sugar. Cut in butter until mixture resembles coarse meal.

Add egg, buttermilk, walnuts and dates. Stir with a fork to make a soft dough. Do not over mix. If dough seems too sticky, add a little more flour.

Drop by 1/4 cupfuls onto a greased sheet. Brush tops with buttermilk. Sprinkle with sugar. Bake about 25 minutes.

Up to 1/2 cup whole wheat flour may be substituted for 1/2 cup of all-purpose flour.

2 cups all-purpose flour
1/4 cup unprocessed wheat bran
2 teaspoons baking powder
1/2 teaspoon baking soda
1 teaspoon salt
2 teaspoons cinnamon
1/4 cup dark brown sugar
1/2 cup chilled butter
1 egg, beaten
2/3 cup buttermilk
1/2 cup chopped walnuts
2/3 cup chopped dates
buttermilk for brushing tops
sugar for sprinkling tops

Preheat oven to 350°

Cookies & Confections

COOKIES

Given the sad state of commercial cookies, homemade cookies are more appreciated than ever.

Perfect cookies are quick and easy to make if you keep these points in mind:

✓ Sift dry ingredients to distribute leavening agents evenly.

✓ The type of shortening used affects texture. We generally prefer butter, which makes slightly crisper cookies.

✓ Mix until dough is well combined. However, you don't have to continue mixing after this point is reached.

✓ Prepare sheets as directed in the recipe. You can substitute parchment paper for greasing (don't use wax paper; it will smolder). Baking sheets usually don't need to be re-greased between trayfuls.

✓ Shiny baking sheets work best. If all your sheets are dark, try covering them with aluminum foil. We love the new "air cushioned" sheets. They produce perfect cookies (no overbaked bottoms) every time. You can try improvising by stacking two ordinary baking sheets together.

✓ We advise against using rimmed baking sheets (jelly roll pans) for cookies. The rim interferes with heat distribution. If you must use them, avoid placing cookies near the edges of the pan.

✓ Leave ample space between cookies to allow room for spreading. If you're not sure how much a new batch will spread, leave 3" between cookies on the first trayful until you know how much room each cookie needs.

✓ Unless otherwise directed, let cookies sit on the baking sheet about 1 minute before removing them with a spatula to a rack in a single layer to cool. Bar cookies are generally cooled in their baking pan on a rack.

✓ Allow baking sheets to cool completely before baking more cookies or the next batch may spread too much.

✓ Allow cookies to cool completely before storing in an airtight bag or container. The least bit of steam will make them soggy. We never met a cookie that didn't freeze well. Thaw them at room temperature and crisp in the oven briefly, if necessary.

BLACK FOREST JUMBLES

3 Dozen Cookies

These rich chocolate drop cookies are packed with hidden surprises.

In a large mixing bowl, cream butter and sugar. Mix in egg and vanilla.

Sift together flour, cocoa, baking powder, baking soda and salt. Add dry ingredients alternately with buttermilk. Stir in oats, cherries and almonds.

Drop by heaping teaspoonfuls on a greased baking sheet, 2" apart.

Bake 8 to 10 minutes until firm to a light touch.

Remove to a wire rack to cool.

1/3 cup butter

1/2 cup sugar

1 egg

1 teaspoon vanilla extract

2/3 cup all-purpose flour

1/2 cup cocoa

1-1/2 teaspoons baking powder

1/2 teaspoon baking soda

1/2 teaspoon salt

1/3 cup buttermilk

2 cups quick-cooking oats

1 cup dried cherries

1/2 cup slivered almonds, toasted

Preheat oven to 375°

BUTTERMILK ALMOND RUM BALLS

About 8 Dozen

4-1/2 cups crushed
vanilla wafers (about
18 ounces)

3/4 cup melted butter

1/3 cup almond paste

1/2 cup buttermilk

1/3 cup cocoa

1-1/2 cups
confectioners sugar

3/4 cup dark rum

8 ounces finely
chopped pecans

*A perennial favorite holiday sweet. This easy
to make confection introduces a new flavor —
almond paste — to the traditional batter.*

In a large mixing bowl, combine all
ingredients. It's that easy!

If you have the time, chill the batter slightly.
It makes the batter easier to roll.

Roll batter into bite-size balls.

Chill balls several hours in the refrigerator. (If
you skip this part, the coating will be
absorbed by the balls.) Roll the balls in cocoa,
confectioners sugar or finely chopped
almonds to coat.

> **Hint**: Grind the wafers in your food
> processor. Empty them out and then
> grind the pecans.

CLASSIC CHOCOLATE CHIP COOKIES

3-1/2 to 4 Dozen Large Cookies

These are a crisp, delicious, buttermilk version of the classic chocolate chip. For chocolate-chocolate chips, add 1/2 cup cocoa to the dry ingredients.

Cream shortening with sugars. Beat in eggs one at a time. Stir in vanilla.

Sift flour with baking soda. Add to creamed mixture alternately with buttermilk. Stir in chocolate chips and pecans.

Drop by slightly heaping tablespoonfuls 3" apart on lightly greased baking sheet.

Bake 15 to 18 minutes until golden brown. Cool on sheet 1 to 2 minutes. Remove to rack to cool completely. Store in airtight container.

1 cup vegetable shortening or butter

1 cup sugar

1 cup dark brown sugar, packed

2 eggs

1-1/2 teaspoons vanilla extract

3 cups all-purpose flour

1 teaspoon baking soda

1/2 cup buttermilk

12 ounces semi-sweet chocolate chips

1 cup coarsely chopped pecans (optional)

Preheat oven to 350°

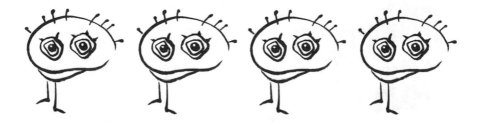

CHOCOLATE FROSTED SMOOCHES

3 Dozen

Cookies:

3 ounces unsweetened chocolate

1/2 cup butter

1 cup dark brown sugar

2 beaten eggs

1 teaspoon vanilla extract

2 cups all-purpose flour

1 teaspoon baking powder

1/2 teaspoon baking soda

1/2 cup buttermilk

Frosting:

1 ounce unsweetened chocolate

2-1/2 cups sifted confectioners sugar

2 tablespoons light cream or milk

1 teaspoon vanilla

Preheat over to 350°

These smooches will kiss your chocolate cravings away.

Cookies:

In a double boiler, melt 3 ounces unsweetened chocolate and butter. Remove from heat. Mix in brown sugar, eggs and vanilla. Turn into a large mixing bowl. Set aside. Leave your double boiler on the stove. You'll need it for the frosting.

Sift together flour, baking powder and baking soda.

Add the dry ingredients to the chocolate mixture, alternately with the buttermilk. Mixture will resemble a cake batter.

Drop by rounded tablespoonfuls 2" apart on an ungreased cookie sheet. Bake 12 minutes, until firm to a light touch. Remove cookies immediately to a wire rack.

Frosting:

Meanwhile, make the frosting:

Melt 1 ounce chocolate in a double boiler. Remove from heat.

In a small bowl, mix confectioners sugar, cream and vanilla. Stir in chocolate until smooth.

Frost cookies while warm.

CRANBERRY HAZELNUT OATMEAL COOKIES

4 to 5 Dozen

A delicate crumbed cookie with the tart taste of cranberries.

Discard any bad cranberries or stems. Cut each cranberry in half. Set aside.

Cream shortening and sugar. Beat in eggs. Sift together flour, baking soda, baking powder, salt, cinnamon and nutmeg. Stir into creamed mixture alternately with buttermilk. Stir in oatmeal, nuts and cranberries.

Drop by heaping teaspoonfuls 2" apart on lightly greased baking sheet. Bake about 10 minutes until dark golden brown. Cool on sheet 1 to 2 minutes. Remove to rack and cool completely.

2 cups fresh or frozen cranberries

1 cup shortening

1-1/2 cups dark brown sugar

2 eggs

2 cups all-purpose flour

1 teaspoon baking soda

1 teaspoon baking powder

1 teaspoon salt

1 teaspoon cinnamon

1 teaspoon freshly grated nutmeg

1/2 cup buttermilk

3 cups quick-cooking oats

3/4 cup finely chopped hazelnuts or pecans

Preheat oven to 375°

GIANT TROPICAL JEWELS

3 Dozen Large Cookies

1 cup vegetable
   shortening

1 teaspoon salt

1 teaspoon baking
   soda

1 teaspoon cinnamon

1 teaspoon ground
   ginger

1 cup sugar

1 beaten egg

1 cup molasses

1/4 cup buttermilk

1 cup diced dried
   mango

1 cup diced dried
   papaya

4 cups all-purpose
   flour

2 cups flaked coconut

Preheat oven to 350°

Dried mangos and papaya are available at most health food stores. Eat these big cookies with a big glass of milk.

In a large mixer bowl, combine shortening, salt, baking soda, cinnamon, ginger and sugar until creamed. Beat in egg, molasses and buttermilk.

Toss mango and papaya with the flour. Stir into creamed mixture until combined. Stir in coconut.

Drop batter by heaping tablespoonfuls about 2" apart on lightly greased baking sheet. Bake 15 minutes or more until just beginning to brown.

Cool on sheet 1 to 2 minutes. Remove cookies to rack to cool completely.

Store cookies in an airtight container with a slice of fresh apple to keep them soft.

KITCHEN SINK OATMEAL COOKIES

More than enough for the next PTA bake sale! If you don't want to make the entire batch at once, any unbaked dough can be refrigerated and baked later.

Cream together butter and sugars. Add eggs and buttermilk. Beat until smooth.

Stir in baking soda, baking powder, salt, cinnamon, nutmeg and vanilla. Beat in flour until well mixed. Stir in oatmeal. Add chocolate chips, nuts, raisins and coconut, and stir until evenly distributed.

Drop by level tablespoonfuls 2" apart on lightly greased baking sheet.

Bake 8 to 10 minutes until just beginning to brown and fairly firm to the touch. Remove immediately to rack to cool. Store these cookies in an airtight container.

1-1/2 cups softened butter

1/2 cup granulated sugar

1-1/2 cups dark brown sugar

3 eggs

3/4 cup buttermilk

1-1/2 teaspoons baking soda

1 teaspoon baking powder

1 teaspoon salt

1 teaspoon cinnamon

1 teaspoon freshly grated nutmeg

1 teaspoon vanilla extract

2 cups all-purpose flour

3 cups quick-cooking oats

12 ounces semi-sweet chocolate chips

1 cup coarsely chopped walnuts or pecans

1/2 cup raisins

1/2 cup flaked coconut

Preheat oven to 375°

MARION'S FRUITCAKE WINKS

3 Dozen Cookies

1/2 cup butter

3/4 cup dark brown sugar

2 eggs, beaten

1-1/2 cups all-purpose flour

1/2 teaspoon baking soda

1 teaspoon cinnamon

1/2 teaspoon ground allspice

1/4 teaspoon freshly grated nutmeg

1/4 teaspoon ground cloves

1/2 teaspoon salt

1/4 cup buttermilk

1/2 teaspoon vanilla, brandy or rum extract

1/2 pound candied cherries, chopped

1/4 pound candied pineapple, chopped

1/4 pound candied lemon peel, chopped

3 cups chopped pecans

The wonderful taste of the holidays without the tedium of making fruitcakes.

Cream together butter and sugar. Beat in eggs. Sift flour with baking soda, cinnamon, allspice, nutmeg, cloves and salt. Add dry ingredients to creamed mixture alternately with buttermilk and vanilla. Stir in candied fruit and pecans.

Drop by heaping tablespoonfuls 2" apart on lightly greased baking sheet.

Bake 25 minutes until bottoms are beginning to brown and cookies are nearly firm to the touch. Remove to rack to cool completely. Cookies will firm on cooling.

Preheat oven to 325°

NORTHWOODS MAPLE FUDGE

9" Square Pan (about 36 pieces)

Butter a 9" square pan well.

In a large saucepan, over medium heat, bring syrup, sugars, baking soda and buttermilk to a boil, stirring to dissolve sugars. Let boil, without stirring, until candy thermometer reaches 236° (soft ball stage — see CARAMEL FROSTING recipe for description of soft ball stage).

Remove from heat. Add butter and vanilla — don't stir. Let it sit in the pan until mixture registers 125°. Beat with a wooden spoon until mixtures thickens and begins to lose its shine. Quickly stir in nuts.

Pour immediately into prepared pan. Let sit for a few minutes. Score fudge. Cool and cut along score lines.

- **1 cup real maple syrup**
- **3 cups dark brown sugar**
- **1 cup granulated sugar**
- **1 teaspoon baking soda**
- **1 cup buttermilk**
- **1 tablespoon butter**
- **2 teaspoons vanilla extract**
- **1/2 cup chopped walnuts (optional)**

MASTER BISCOTTI DOUGH

2 Dozen Cookies

4 cups all-purpose
   flour

1 cup sugar

1 teaspoon salt

2 teaspoons baking
   powder

1/2 cup melted butter

2 beaten eggs

1 teaspoon vanilla
   extract

3/4 cup buttermilk

BISCOTTI
   FLAVORING
   ADDITIONS

Preheat oven to 400°

The name of these classic Italian cookies, biscotti, means "twice cooked". The double-baking process and low fat result in an intentionally dry, crisp cookie that keeps for a long time.

This recipe is unflavored. See BISCOTTI FLAVORING ADDITIONS for flavorings.

In a large mixing bowl, combine flour, sugar, salt and baking powder. Stir in butter, eggs, vanilla, buttermilk and flavoring additions until a moist, soft dough (similar to biscuit dough) forms.

Turn dough out on a dry, floured surface. Divide in two. Pat into 4" x 12" rectangles, 1/2" thick.

Bake on a greased baking sheet 25 minutes. Remove from oven and reduce oven temperature to 200°.

Transfer loaves to a cutting board. With a serrated knife, slice on a slight diagonal into 1" wide slices.

Place cookies directly on oven rack. Bake for about 2 hours until biscotti are dry and crisp.

Any of these flavor combinations can be complemented by dipping the flat side of the biscotti in 4 ounces of quality chocolate melted in a double boiler.

ORANGE LEMON HAZELNUT BISCOTTI
1 teaspoon vanilla extract
3/4 teaspoon almond extract
zest of one lemon
zest of one orange
1 cup toasted hazelnuts

ALMOND BISCOTTI
2 teaspoons vanilla extract
2 teaspoons almond extract
1 cup toasted slivered almonds

ANISE BISCOTTI
1 teaspoon vanilla extract
2 teaspoons anise extract

CHERRY ALMOND BISCOTTI
2 teaspoons vanilla extract
2 teaspoons almond extract
1 cup coarsely chopped dried cherries

CHOCOLATE CHIP BISCOTTI
2 teaspoons vanilla extract
1 cup miniature semi-sweet chocolate morsels

LEMON POPPY SEED BISCOTTI
2 teaspoons lemon extract
grated zest of one lemon
1/2 cup poppy seeds

WALNUT FIG BISCOTTI
1 teaspoon vanilla extract
1 teaspoon lemon extract
3/4 cup diced dried figs
1 cup toasted, coarsely chopped walnuts

CRANBERRY HAZELNUT BISCOTTI
1 teaspoon vanilla extract
1 teaspoon orange extract
grated zest of one orange
1/2 cup halved cranberries

PECAN BISCOTTI
substitute 1/2 cup dark brown sugar for 1/2 cup sugar
2 cups toasted, coarsely chopped pecans

TROPICAL BISCOTTI
1 teaspoon vanilla extract
1 teaspoon rum extract
1/2 cup diced dried mango
1/2 cup diced dried papaya
1/2 cup diced dried pineapple
1/2 cup coarsely chopped macadamia nuts

PLAIN OL' SUGAR COOKIES

8 Dozen

1 cup sugar

1/2 cup butter

1 egg

1 teaspoon vanilla
extract

2 teaspoons baking
powder

3 cups all-purpose
flour

1 teaspoon baking
soda

1/2 cup buttermilk

Preheat oven to 425°

We like these plain without any extra sugar or glaze, but they are also a good cookie for decorating.

In a large mixing bowl, cream together sugar and butter. Stir in egg and vanilla. Sift together baking powder, flour and baking soda. Add dry ingredients alternately with buttermilk, to creamed mixture.

Form two 2" diameter rolls of dough. Wrap in wax paper. Refrigerate several hours or overnight. Slice 1/2" thick and place 2" apart on a greased baking sheet.

Bake 5 to 7 minutes until golden. Check the cookies frequently near the end of baking time to avoid burning.

Cool on sheets for 1 to 2 minutes. Remove to wire rack to cool completely.

RUM RUNNERS MOLASSES DROPS

2-1/2 Dozen

Gingerbread cookies on the wild side! For tamer cookies, plump the raisins in water instead of rum.

Soak raisins in rum at least 1 hour, stirring occasionally. Drain, reserving rum.

In large mixer bowl, cream shortening, sugar and molasses. Stir in buttermilk, rum extract and rum. Mixture may look curdled.

Mix together baking soda, salt, ginger, cinnamon and flour. Stir into creamed mixture until well combined. Add raisins.

Drop cookies by heaping teaspoonfuls about 2" apart on lightly greased baking sheet. Bake about 15 minutes until just starting to brown.

Cool on sheets for 1 to 2 minutes. Remove to wire rack to cool completely.

3/4 cup raisins

about 3 tablespoons dark rum

1/2 cup vegetable shortening

1/2 cup dark brown sugar

1/2 cup molasses

1/2 cup buttermilk

1/2 teaspoon rum extract

2 teaspoons rum reserved from raisins

1 teaspoon baking soda

1/2 teaspoon salt

1/2 teaspoon ground ginger

1/2 teaspoon cinnamon

2-1/2 cups all-purpose flour

Preheat oven to 350°

SEMI-SWEET FLORENTINES

3-1/2 Dozen Cookies

Cookies:
2/3 cup butter, melted
2 cups quick-cooking oats
1 cup sugar
2/3 cup all-purpose flour
1/4 cup light corn syrup
1/4 cup buttermilk
1 teaspoon vanilla extract
1/4 teaspoon salt

Filling:
4 ounces semi-sweet chocolate

Preheat oven to 375°

A grown-up cookie. These sophisticated wafers will elicit a chorus of "You made these yourself?"

Cookies:

In a large mixing bowl, combine butter, oats, sugar, flour, corn syrup, buttermilk, vanilla and salt.

Drop by heaping teaspoonfuls 3" apart on baking sheet lined with aluminum foil. Flatten cookie dough by patting with your fingers.

Bake 6 to 8 minutes until lightly golden. Edges will be slightly darker. Cool completely on baking sheets on wire rack. Peel foil from cookies when completely cooled.

Filling:

Melt semi-sweet chocolate in a double boiler until smooth.

Spread chocolate on flat side of half the batch of cookies. Top with remaining cookies, pressing flat sides onto the chocolate.

S'MORE BROWNIES

These new-fangled fudgie brownies are a gooey, yummy combination of old-fashioned flavors.

Brownies:

In a double boiler, melt butter with cocoa until smooth. Remove from heat. Stir in sugar, egg, flour, buttermilk and vanilla.

Pour mixture into a greased 8" square pan.

Bake 25 minutes until brownie tests done. Do not over-bake or you will dry out the brownies.

Topping:

Combine marshmallows, walnuts, chocolate and butterscotch morsels. Sprinkle on top of brownies and return to oven for 3 to 5 minutes, just long enough for topping to begin to melt together.

Cool in pan on wire rack before cutting into squares. These are a little tricky to get out of the pan.

Brownies:
1/2 cup butter
1/2 cup cocoa
1 cup sugar
1 egg
1/2 cup all-purpose flour
1/4 cup buttermilk
1 teaspoon vanilla extract

Topping:
2/3 cup miniature marshmallows
1/2 cup coarsely chopped walnuts
1/2 cup semi-sweet chocolate morsels
1/2 cup butterscotch morsels

Preheat oven to 350°

SOFT HERMIT BARS

18 Bar Cookies

1 cup sugar
1/2 cup butter
1/2 cup molasses
3 cups all-purpose
flour
1 teaspoon cinnamon
1/2 teaspoon freshly
grated nutmeg
1/2 teaspoon salt
1 teaspoon baking
soda
1/2 cup buttermilk
1/2 cup molasses

Preheat oven to 350°

These are a traditional New England treat. For a simple dessert, warm the cookies in a toaster oven and top with vanilla ice cream and chocolate sauce.

In a large mixing bowl, cream together butter and sugar. Add molasses. Sift together flour, cinnamon, nutmeg, salt and baking soda. Add dry ingredients, alternately with buttermilk, to creamed mixture to make a stiff dough.

Spread on greased 15" x 10" jelly roll pan. Batter will spread to the edges of the pan during baking.

Bake 20 to 25 minutes until bars test done. Place pan on wire rack to cool. Cut into squares when cool, trimming off thin or dark edges.

SUNSHINE BARS

These delicately flavored petits four-like bars are the perfect accompaniment to a quiet cup of tea.

Bars:

In a large mixing bowl, beat sugar and butter until light and fluffy. Add the molasses and egg. Beat well.

Sift together flour, baking soda and ginger. Add to creamed mixture alternately with the buttermilk. Mix well.

Stir in nuts and zest.

Spread in greased 10" x 15" jelly roll pan.

Bake 15 to 20 minutes until tests done. Cool in pan on wire rack.

Icing:

Meanwhile, prepare the icing: Beat the sugar, butter, zest and orange juice until smooth.

Trim browned edges from cooled cookies. Spread with icing. Cut into 3" x 1" bars.

Bars:
1/2 cup sugar
1/2 cup softened butter
1/2 cup molasses
1 egg
2 cups all-purpose flour
1 teaspoon baking soda
1 teaspoon ground ginger
2/3 cup buttermilk
1/2 cup chopped walnuts
2 teaspoons orange zest

Icing:
3 cups sifted confectioners sugar
3 tablespoons softened butter
1 teaspoon orange zest
5 to 6 tablespoons fresh-squeezed orange juice

Preheat oven to 350°

Cheesecakes, Pies & Frozen Delights

CHOCOLATE MOCHA CHEESECAKE

9" Cheesecake

A velvety smooth, rich chocolate torte.

Crust:

Mix cookie crumbs, sugar and butter. Press into bottom of a greased 9" springform pan.

Filling:

In a double boiler, melt chocolate and butter. Set aside.

In a large mixing bowl, cream together cream cheese and sugar. Add chocolate-butter mixture, vanilla, espresso, buttermilk, cocoa and flour. Mix well. Beat in the eggs until just mixed.

Pour mixture carefully into crust.

Bake about 30 minutes until set. Cool in pan. Remove rim and chill.

Crust:

1-1/2 cups chocolate wafer or chocolate graham cracker crumbs

1/4 cup sugar

3 tablespoons melted butter

Filling:

3 ounces quality unsweetened or semi-sweet chocolate

1/4 cup butter

8 ounces softened cream cheese

1/2 cup sugar

1 teaspoon vanilla extract

1/2 cup strong-brewed espresso (instant espresso works fine)

1/2 cup buttermilk

3 tablespoons cocoa

2 tablespoons flour

2 eggs

Preheat oven to 325°

PUMPKIN PECAN CHEESECAKE

9" Cheesecake

Crust:

1-1/2 cups gingersnap
  crumbs

1/4 cup sugar

3 tablespoons melted
  butter

1/2 cup finely chopped
  pecans

Filling:

8 ounces softened
  cream cheese

1/2 cup real maple
  syrup or dark brown
  sugar

1 teaspoon vanilla
  extract

1/4 cup sugar

1-1/2 teaspoons
  cinnamon

1/2 teaspoon freshly
  grated nutmeg

1/4 teaspoon ground
  ginger

1/4 teaspoon ground
  cloves

1 cup pumpkin puree

1/2 cup buttermilk

2 tablespoons flour

2 eggs

real maple syrup for
  glaze

8 pecan halves for
  decoration

Preheat oven to 325°

Pumpkin pie pales in comparison.

Crust:

Mix cookie crumbs, sugar, butter and pecans. Press into bottom of a greased 9" springform pan.

Filling:

In a large mixing bowl, cream together cream cheese, maple syrup, vanilla and sugar. Add cinnamon, nutmeg, ginger, cloves, pumpkin, buttermilk and flour. Mix well. Beat in the eggs, just until mixed.

Pour mixture carefully into crust.

Bake about 40 minutes until set. Cool in pan. Brush with maple syrup. Decorate with whole pecans.

Remove rim and chill.

BUTTERMILK BREAD PUDDING with BUTTERSCOTCH SAUCE

4 to 6 Servings

Traditionally a thrifty use for slightly stale bread, this is especially good when stale cake or doughnuts are substituted for the bread.

Pudding:

Butter a 9" x 5" loaf pan.

Sprinkle bread cubes with baking soda. Pour buttermilk over bread and let stand 15 minutes. Mix butter, sugar and egg well. Add cinnamon and nutmeg. Pour over bread cubes. Stir gently to combine. Fold in raisins gently. Spread evenly in prepared pan. Cover pan with foil. Bake 30 minutes. Uncover and bake an additional 30 minutes. Serve hot with warm sauce.

Sauce:

In a 3-quart saucepan, stir sugar, butter, baking soda, buttermilk and corn syrup over medium heat until sugar dissolves. Bring to a full boil and boil 10 minutes. Remove from heat. Stir in vanilla. Store unused sauce in refrigerator.

Pudding:

2 cups 1" or smaller bread cubes

1 teaspoon baking soda

1 cup buttermilk

1 tablespoon butter

1/2 cup sugar

1 egg, beaten

3/4 teaspoon cinnamon

1/4 teaspoon freshly grated nutmeg

1/2 cup raisins or other small dried fruit

Sauce:

1 cup sugar

4 ounces butter

1/2 teaspoon baking soda

1/2 cup buttermilk

1/4 cup white corn syrup

1 teaspoon vanilla

Preheat oven to 350°

BUTTERMILK PIE CRUST

1 Double 9" Crust

2 cups all-purpose
  flour
1 tablespoon sugar
1/4 teaspoon salt
1-1/2 sticks butter, cut
  into tablespoon-size
  pieces
1/3 cup buttermilk

This crust works up like a dream. The buttermilk yields a light, flaky crust for pies, tarts and quiches.

In a large mixing bowl, combine flour, sugar and salt. Cut in butter until mixture resembles coarse meal. Add buttermilk and mix only until moistened.

Divide dough in half and form into two disks. Wrap individually in wax paper and refrigerate for 15 minutes.

Roll pastry between two sheets of lightly floured wax paper.

BUTTERMILK RAISIN PIE

9" Pie

1 recipe
  BUTTERMILK PIE
  CRUST
grated zest of 1 lemon
3 cups raisins
3 eggs, reserving 1 egg
  white for wash
1 cup buttermilk
1 teaspoon lemon
  extract
1/2 cup sugar
2 tablespoons instant
  tapioca
1/2 teaspoon salt

Preheat oven to 375°

Serve this pie for a special breakfast treat or as a classic "comfort" dessert. This pie tastes best warm.

Prepare BUTTERMILK PIE CRUST, adding lemon zest to flour.

Cover raisins with boiling water to plump.

Beat together eggs, buttermilk and lemon extract. Add sugar, tapioca and salt. Stir in drained raisins.

Pour mixture into pastry-lined 9" pie pan. Add top crust. Crimp edges. Cut vents in pie. Wash with reserved egg white. Cover crimped edges with narrow strips of aluminum foil.

Bake for 45 to 50 minutes, removing foil during the last 15 minutes of baking.

For ORANGE BUTTERMILK RAISIN PIE, substitute orange extract and orange zest for lemon.

COCONUT PIE

This is a very pretty pie, packed with coconut.

In a large mixing bowl, combine sugar, butter, eggs, buttermilk, vanilla and coconut. Pour into unbaked pie shell. Bake one hour until custard is set.

1-1/2 cups sugar
1/4 cup melted butter
4 well beaten eggs
1/2 cup buttermilk
1 teaspoon vanilla
  extract
2 cups flaked coconut
1/2 recipe
  BUTTERMILK PIE
  CRUST

Preheat oven to 325°

LEMON CUSTARD PIE

9" Pie

The color of sunshine with a refreshing lemon taste.

In large mixing bowl, mix sugar, flour and nutmeg. Add butter. Beat until creamy. Stir in eggs, buttermilk, lemon juice, vanilla and zest. Pour into unbaked pie shell. Sprinkle with nutmeg.

Bake for 10 minutes at 400°. Reduce heat to 325°. Bake for 30 minutes or until set.

2 cups sugar
3 tablespoons flour
1/4 teaspoon freshly
  grated nutmeg
1/4 cup melted butter
4 eggs, well beaten
1 cup buttermilk
1/4 cup fresh lemon
  juice
1 teaspoon vanilla
  extract
zest of one lemon
1/2 recipe
  BUTTERMILK PIE
  CRUST
nutmeg for sprinkling

Preheat oven to 400°

CAPE COD SMOOTHIE

1 Quart

1/2 cup orange juice
1-1/2 cups sugar
1 teaspoon grated orange zest
2 cups fresh or frozen whole cranberries
1-1/2 cups buttermilk
1 teaspoon orange or lemon extract

This chiffon-like sherbet has a beautiful crimson color and a tangy-sweet taste.

In a medium size, heavy saucepan, bring orange juice, sugar and zest to a boil, stirring to dissolve sugar. Boil 5 minutes.

Add cranberries. Lower heat and simmer 10 minutes, stirring occasionally, until berries are popped and sauce is slightly thickened.

Remove from heat and cool to room temperature. Puree mixture in a blender or food processor until smooth. Stir in buttermilk and extract. Chill overnight.

Process in an ice cream maker according to manufacturer's instructions. Transfer to an airtight container and freeze until firm.

> If you don't have an ice cream maker, pour mixture into a metal loaf pan or bowl. Freeze until partially frozen. Beat with a mixer or food processor. Freeze until nearly firm. Beat again. Freeze until firm.

CHOCOLATE TOASTED ALMOND ICE CREAM

1 Quart

To show off the wonderful textures of this dessert, layer with fresh whipped cream in tulip glasses.

In a small bowl, cream egg yolks and sugar. Set aside.

In a medium saucepan, over medium heat, bring cream to a simmer. Temper egg mixture by stirring in about 1/2 cup hot cream. Stir tempered egg mixture into remaining cream.

Stir constantly until mixture coats the back of a wooden spoon. Remove from heat. Whisk in chocolate and buttermilk. Stir in extract.

Chill mixture overnight.

Process in ice cream maker according to manufacturer's instructions. Stir in almonds. Transfer to an airtight container and freeze until firm.

4 egg yolks

1 cup sugar

2-1/2 cups light cream

7 ounces semi-sweet chocolate, chopped

1 cup buttermilk

1 teaspoon almond extract

1/3 cup unblanched almonds, toasted

LEMON BUTTERMILK CHIFFON SHERBET

1 Quart

3/4 cup sugar
1/2 cup fresh lemon
 juice
6 egg yolks
2 cups buttermilk
zest of 1 lemon

A lemon and buttermilk lovers' delight.

In a medium-size heavy saucepan, whisk together sugar, lemon juice and egg yolks.

Over moderate heat, whisking constantly, cook mixture (do not allow to boil) about 15 minutes or until candy thermometer registers 175°.

Combine cooked mixture, buttermilk and lemon zest. Chill overnight.

Process in ice cream maker according to manufacturer's instructions. Transfer to an airtight container and freeze until firm.

MANGO MAMBO SHERBET

1 Quart

2/3 cup sugar
1 cup water
dash of salt
3 medium, ripe
 mangos, peeled and
 sliced, or
26-ounce jar of sliced
 mangos, reserve
 liquid
1 tablespoon lemon
 juice
1/4 cup buttermilk
1/4 cup water or
 reserved liquid

A very refreshing, light dessert.

In a medium-size saucepan, combine water, sugar and salt. Cook over medium heat 10 to 15 minutes until sugar is dissolved. Set aside.

In a food processor or blender, puree lemon juice, mangos and water or reserved liquid until smooth. Stir in sugar mixture. Chill overnight.

Process in an ice cream maker according to manufacturer's instructions. Transfer to an airtight container and freeze until firm.

MAUI SHERBET

1 Quart

As delicious as a moonlight stroll on the beach.

Place buttermilk, sugar, salt, pineapple, vanilla and egg yolk in a food processor or blender. Process until nearly smooth.

Transfer mixture to medium-size bowl. Add coconut.

Fold in egg white. Egg white need not be completely incorporated.

Process in ice cream maker according to manufacturer's instructions. Transfer to an airtight container and freeze until firm.

2 cups buttermilk
2/3 cup sugar
dash of salt
8-ounce can undrained crushed pineapple
2 teaspoons vanilla extract
1 egg yolk
1/3 cup flaked coconut
1 egg white, beaten until stiff

THE FROZEN PUMPKIN PATCH

1 Quart

Add the bourbon at the very last moment of processing. If the alcohol is added too soon, the mixture will not set up.

In a medium saucepan, whisk together buttermilk, eggs and sugar. Over medium heat, bring to a simmer until mixture coats the back of a wooden spoon. Remove from heat.

Whisk in pumpkin, light cream, nutmeg and cinnamon. Chill mixture overnight.

Process in ice cream maker according to manufacturer's instructions. Add bourbon at end of processing. Transfer to an airtight container and freeze until firm.

1 cup buttermilk
2 eggs
1/2 cup sugar
1 cup pumpkin puree
1-1/2 cups light cream
3/4 teaspoon freshly grated nutmeg
1/2 teaspoon cinnamon
1 tablespoon bourbon

Yeast Breads

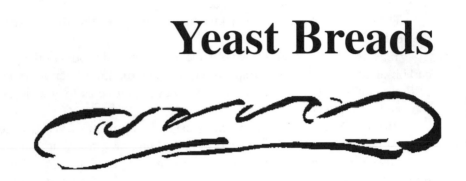

FEAR of RISING:
All you really need to know about yeast-leavened bread

Many cooks hesitate to make yeast breads because they think it's either too difficult or too time-consuming. But you can make wonderful breads easily in just about any time frame. The process is very forgiving and can be manipulated to suit any schedule. It is also one of the most rewarding of cooking experiences.

The one critical element in making successful yeast breads is to keep the yeast alive.

Yeast is a living organism which digests sugars and produces the gas, carbon dioxide, which, when trapped within the structure of certain types of flours, inflates it. Yeast will be happy and productive as long as it has food and an ambient temperature.

PROOFING is the first and most crucial step in most yeast bread recipes. Proofing means testing yeast to make sure, or "prove," it's alive.

Most yeast bread recipes begin with stirring the yeast into some warm liquid with a bit of sugar to provide immediate food for the yeast. Within minutes, the mixture begins to foam slightly and smell yeasty. If the yeast shows no signs of activity within 10 minutes or so, it was either too old or you may have killed it because the liquid was too hot. If the liquid was too cold, the yeast will be sluggish or even appear dormant. If you're using bulk yeast without instructions, use liquids at about 110° (***HINT***: *heat some water to 110° using a thermometer. Put your finger in it. From here on in, you'll know how it should feel*). Otherwise, follow the manufacturer's directions on the packaging.

Active dry yeast was a wonderful development. It allows you to store your yeast until you need it — well, almost. It does have a shelf life and it does expire, literally. One scant tablespoon of bulk yeast is the equivalent of a standard 1/4-ounce packet of yeast. Bulk yeast is by far the best buy if you plan to make bread fairly often. Store it in an airtight container in your refrigerator, making a note of the expiration date that appears on the original package.

Yeast's sensitivity to temperature is an asset that allows you to manage your bread making to fit your schedule. We'll discuss this after kneading.

After proofing the yeast, a bread recipe will generally instruct you to add such things as a fat, salt, additional sweetener or flavorings. Although each of these plays a role in the texture and flavor of the final loaf, you may omit or change them to fit your personal preferences. Then you will be

---

adding flour. Wheat flour generally provides the gluten for the structure that captures the gases given off by the yeast. Different types of wheat flour have different amounts of gluten. Generally, bread flour (made from hard wheat) has the most; all-purpose and whole wheat flours have an adequate amount; and cake, biscuit or pastry flour lack an adequate amount of gluten for bread. Many other "flours," such as buckwheat and barley, lack any gluten and can be used only as a portion of the flour.

Some recipes use the "sponge method," where only a part of the flour is added and the dough is allowed to rise before the remaining portion is used. Other recipes instruct you to add all or most of the flour before rising. Once you have added most of the flour, your are ready to knead.

KNEADING is a key element in determining the texture of the finished loaf. If you have a heavy-duty stand mixer, you can have the machine knead the bread right in the mixing bowl, using the dough hook which came with your mixer. Otherwise, lightly flour a dry surface at least 12" square, and turn out the dough. Sprinkle it lightly with flour and work it with the heels of your hands, pushing it forward, then pulling the far edge toward you. Continue this motion at least five minutes (preferably longer), adding a little more flour if needed, until the dough is smooth and forms a coherent — yes, it does feel like a baby's bottom — mass. Shape dough into a ball and place in a large greased, oiled or buttered bowl. Turn the dough so it is coated with the fat to keep the dough from drying out and forming hard bits that won't be fully incorporated into the loaf. Loosely cover the rising dough with a clean dish towel.

RISING: Yeast-leavened breads need at least one "rising" to give the yeast organisms a chance to create the carbon dioxide that gives the bread its structure. Most breads require and benefit by additional risings. Recipes usually call for two risings. Consider this the minimum. Place dough in a draft-free environment to rise. We like to use the top of the refrigerator. The bread can be punched down (expelling the yeast-produced gas) and allowed to rise two or three additional times if you aren't ready to bake it. Or you can place the dough in the refrigerator to retard rising by many hours or even a day or two. Allow it about three hours to return to room temperature before proceeding. Do not, however, let the dough rise more than about double its original size or the texture will be adversely affected. Raw bread dough can also be frozen for short periods, but it's better to freeze the baked loaf instead.

SHAPING and BAKING: Bread can be baked in a greased pan or shaped in rounds or oblongs (or even more artistic designs) and baked on a greased flat surface like a baking sheet or stone preferably sprinkled with cornmeal. In most recipes, the dough is then allowed to rise once more.

Breads can be glazed or washed a number of ways after their final risings, each resulting in a different crust characteristic:

✓ Beaten whole egg or yolk makes a dark and shiny final crust.

✓ Beaten egg white darkens the crust to a lesser degree.

✓ Milk helps the crust darken and be a bit softer.

✓ Water encourages a crunchier crust.

✓ Butter softens the crust and is often spread on bread just after it is taken from the oven.

✓ Glazes are optional for most loaves, but they are a necessity if you plan to use a topping like salt, seeds, herbs, onions, sugar, etc., because they act as the "glue" to keep these additions attached to the loaf. Raised loaves may also be slashed with a sharp knife or razor, or dusted with flour for a more artistic appearance.

Preheat the oven to the temperature suggested by the recipe. For a crustier loaf, place a pan of hot water on the lowest oven shelf or mist the oven a few times during the initial 20 minutes of baking.

IS IT BREAD YET? Testing for doneness is more of an art than a science. Experience may be the best teacher, but here are a few hints. Bread is done when:

✓ It has a golden brown color and crisp exterior (glazed breads will generally be darker than unglazed loaves).

✓ It sounds hollow when tapped on the bottom.

✓ An instant-read thermometer thrust into the loaf reads 190°.

Overbaking, in our opinion, is preferable to underbaking, with a thicker crust the only possible drawback.

CUTTING BREAD: Every bread book will tell you to cool your loaves completely before slicing. We say, "GET REAL." You'll want to cut it as soon as it comes out of the oven. Hot bread should be cut with a serrated bread knife using very slight pressure. Piping hot bread with butter — pure heaven.

BASIC WHITE BREAD

In a small saucepan over medium heat, warm buttermilk and butter. Butter need not be totally melted. Cool to lukewarm.

In a large mixing bowl, combine buttermilk-butter mixture, yeast and sugar. Proof yeast until foamy, about 10 minutes. Stir in salt.

Immediately add bread flour. Knead well on a floured surface until smooth and elastic.

Turn in a greased bowl. Cover and let rise until doubled, about 1 hour.

Grease two 8" x 4" loaf pans.

Punch down dough and shape into 2 smooth, oblong loaves. Place in prepared loaf pans. Cover and let rise 50 to 60 minutes. Apply wash if desired.

Bake 40 to 45 minutes until golden brown and tests done.

Turn bread out onto a wire rack to cool.

2 cups buttermilk
1/2 cup butter, cut in small pieces
1 packet active dry yeast
3 tablespoons sugar
2 teaspoons salt
6 cups bread flour

Preheat oven to 375°

> To crisp the sides and bottoms of pan-baked loaves, turn them out of the pan and place them directly on the oven rack for the last 5 minutes or so of baking.

BUTTERMILK BAGELS

12 Large Bagels

1 cup buttermilk

1/4 cup butter

2 tablespoons sugar

1/2 teaspoon salt

1 packet active dry
yeast

1 egg

3-3/4 cups all-purpose
flour

cornmeal for dusting

2 tablespoons honey

1 egg yolk

1 teaspoon water

poppy seeds, sesame
seeds, dried onion or
garlic flakes or
coarse salt (optional)

Preheat oven to 400°

Bagels get their chewy crusts from boiling before baking.

Heat the buttermilk, butter, sugar and salt until butter melts. Mixture may curdle. Cool to lukewarm. Stir in yeast and egg. Let mixture proof until foamy, about 10 minutes. Beat in flour.

Knead on floured surface 5 to 10 minutes until dough is smooth and elastic. Place in greased bowl and turn to coat dough. Cover and let double, about 1 hour. Divide dough into 12 balls. Shape each ball into a bagel by forcing your fingers into center of ball and stretching to form a doughnut shape. Place on floured surface and let rest, uncovered, about 10 minutes.

Grease a large baking sheet and dust with cornmeal.

Meanwhile, bring a large pot of water to a boil. Add honey. Reduce heat so water simmers gently. Drop bagels into water one at a time. Cook 30 seconds. Turn and cook an additional 30 seconds. Remove bagels with slotted spoon to prepared sheet, leaving about 2" between bagels. Mix egg yolk and water. Brush on bagels. Sprinkle with optional topping(s) if desired. Bake about 20 minutes until browned and crisp.

DAIRY CHALLAH

2 Large Loaves

*Challah is the traditional bread eaten by
many Jewish families at the Sabbath dinner.
Peoples of all faiths love this eggy, slightly
sweet bread for French toast.*

*See our recipe for BUTTERMILK FRENCH
TOAST.*

In a large mixing bowl, dissolve yeast in
water. Proof yeast until foamy, about 10
minutes.

In a separate bowl, beat eggs, reserving about
2 tablespoons for glaze.

Add butter, buttermilk, sugar, salt and eggs to
yeast mixture. Mix well.

Stir in 6-1/2 cups flour. Turn out on dry,
floured surface and knead in additional flour
as necessary until dough does not stick to
floured hands. Knead until smooth and
clastic, about 10 minutes. Knead in raisins
during last 2 minutes.

Turn dough in buttered bowl. Cover. Let
double, about 1 hour.

Grease a large baking sheet.

Punch down and shape dough in two rounds.
Place seam down on prepared baking sheet.
Cover and let rise until doubled, about 45
minutes. Brush with reserved egg wash.

Bake about 40 minutes until golden and
brown and tests done. Turn bread out on wire
rack to cool.

2 packets dry yeast
1/2 cup warm water
3 eggs
6 tablespoons melted
butter
1-1/2 cups room-
temperature
buttermilk
3 tablespoons sugar
2 teaspoons salt
about 7 cups bread
flour
1-1/2 cups golden
raisins (optional)

Preheat oven to 375 °

For an easy version of the traditional braided challah shape, divide
each portion of dough into three pieces. Roll out like a snake. Pinch
edges together and braid. Continue with second rising as directed
above.

DILLED FETA CHEESE BREAD

1 Large Loaf

1/2 cup lukewarm
water

1/2 cup room-
temperature
buttermilk

1 tablespoon extra-
virgin olive oil

1-1/2 teaspoons sugar

1 packet dry yeast

2-1/2 cups bread flour

4 tablespoons fresh
dill or 2 tablespoons
dried dill

1-1/2 cups crumbled
feta cheese, patted
dry

cornmeal for dusting

Preheat oven to 375°

Opaa! Share the joys of the Greek Isles with this luscious loaf.

In large mixing bowl, combine water, buttermilk, oil, sugar and yeast. Proof yeast until foamy, about 10 minutes.

Beat in flour and dill, adding a little more flour if needed.

Knead on floured surface 5 to 10 minutes until dough is smooth and elastic. Knead in feta cheese. This dough will be a little softer than most bread doughs. Place in an olive oiled bowl. Turn dough to coat.

Cover and let rise until doubled, about 45 to 55 minutes.

Grease a baking sheet and dust with cornmeal.

Punch down dough and shape into round or oblong loaf. Place seam down on prepared baking sheet. Cover and let double again, about 30 to 40 minutes.

Apply a wash if desired.

Place a pan of very hot water on the bottom or bottom shelf of oven. Bake 35 minutes until bread is golden and tests done. Turn bread out on a wire rack to cool.

FAUX-CACCIA

15" Flat Bread

Focaccia is an Italian flat bread. A cousin to pizza, the flavors in this bread come more from the dough than the toppings. Feel free to experiment with your favorite herbs and spices.

In a large bowl, mix buttermilk, yeast and sugar. Proof the yeast until foamy, about 10 minutes.

Stir in semolina flour, salt, rosemary, 3 tablespoons olive oil and water. Mix in flour to make a soft dough.

Knead on a well-floured surface, adding additional flour if necessary. Continue kneading 5 to 10 minutes until dough is smooth and elastic. Dough will be soft.

Place in an olive-oiled bowl, turning once to coat dough. Cover and let rise, about 60 minutes, until doubled.

Meanwhile, sauté onion in 2 tablespoons of olive oil until just softened.

Cover a 15" x 10" jelly roll pan with aluminum foil. Wipe with olive oil and dust with cornmeal.

Punch down dough and spread evenly to cover the pan. Spread with onion mixture. Dot with olives and drizzle with 1 tablespoon olive oil.

Bake 20 minutes or until golden brown.

1/2 cup room-temperature buttermilk
1 packet active dry yeast
pinch of sugar
1 cup semolina flour
2 teaspoons salt
1 teaspoon dried, crushed rosemary
3 tablespoons extra-virgin olive oil
1 cup lukewarm water
3 cups white bread flour
1/2 cup sliced onion
3 tablespoons extra-virgin olive oil, divided
cornmeal for dusting
10 to 15 pitted and halved kalamata olives

Preheat oven to 450°

HONEY BUCKWHEAT CURRANT BROWN BREAD

2 Small Loaves

1/2 cup lukewarm water

2 packets active dry yeast

1 tablespoon sugar

1 cup buckwheat flour

2 tablespoons cocoa

2 teaspoons salt

1 cup buttermilk

1/4 cup molasses

1/4 cup honey

2 tablespoons vegetable oil

3-1/2 cups bread flour

3/4 cup dried currants

Preheat oven to 350°

In a large mixing bowl, mix water, yeast and sugar. Proof yeast until foamy, about 10 minutes. Stir in buckwheat flour, cocoa and salt. Stir in buttermilk, molasses, honey and oil. Mix in 3 cups bread flour.

Knead well on a floured surface, incorporating currants and at least 1/2 cup more bread flour to make soft, slightly sticky dough.

Turn in a greased bowl. Cover and let rise until doubled, about 75 minutes. Punch down.

Grease two 8" x 4" loaf pans.

Divide dough in half and shape into 2 oblong loaves. Place in prepared pans. Cover and let double, about 1 hour.

Apply wash if desired.

Bake 50 to 60 minutes until bread tests done. Turn out on wire rack to cool.

MAPLE-KISSED BUTTERMILK BREAD

2 Loaves

A slightly sweet, sturdy white bread with a tender crust.

Combine buttermilk, butter, maple syrup and salt in a small saucepan. Heat on low until butter is nearly melted. Cool to lukewarm.

Stir in yeast and let proof until foamy, about 10 minutes. Add egg. Beat in 6 cups flour, adding additional flour, if needed, to make slightly sticky dough. Knead well on floured surface until smooth and elastic.

Turn in greased bowl. Cover and let rise until doubled, about 1 hour. Punch down.

Grease two 9" x 5" loaf pans.

Shape in 2 oblong loaves and place in prepared pans or shape in rounds on greased sheets sprinkled with cornmeal. Cover and let rise until doubled, about 45 minutes.

Bake 50 minutes or longer until golden brown and tests done. Turn out on wire rack to cool.

2 cups buttermilk
1/4 cup butter
1/2 cup real maple syrup
1/2 teaspoon salt
1 packet dry yeast
1 beaten egg
6 to 6-1/2 cups all-purpose flour
(or substitute up to 3 cups of whole wheat flour for a heartier loaf)

Preheat oven to 350°

MIDNIGHT SUN RYE BREAD

2 Loaves

2 packets active dry
  yeast
pinch of sugar
1 cup lukewarm water
1 tablespoon salt
1 tablespoon sugar
1 tablespoon fennel
  seeds
2 packed tablespoons
  grated orange zest
1 cup buttermilk
2 ounces melted
  butter, cooled to
  room temperature
2 cups rye flour
3 cups bread flour
cornmeal for dusting

Preheat oven to 375°

This is a buttermilk version of classic Finnish rye bread. The orange zest and fennel seeds give this rye loaf a subtle change of taste.

In large mixing bowl, combine yeast, pinch of sugar and water. Proof yeast until foamy, about 10 minutes.

Stir in salt, 1 tablespoon sugar, fennel seeds and orange zest. Add buttermilk, butter and rye flour. Stir well. Work in bread flour. Knead well on floured surface until smooth and elastic.

Turn in greased bowl. Cover and let rise until doubled, about 1 hour. Punch down. If time permits, let rise a second time.

Grease a large baking sheet and dust with cornmeal.

Shape dough into 2 oblongs or rounds. Place seam down on prepared sheet. Cover and let rise until doubled, about 45 minutes.

Apply a wash if desired.

Bake 40 minutes or longer until golden brown and tests done. Turn loaves out on a wire rack to cool.

ONION SAGE ROLLS

16 Rolls

Anna's seven-year-old son, Bubba, doesn't like to eat anything, but he loves these rolls.

In a medium-size skillet, sauté onion in 2 tablespoons butter until lightly browned. Set aside.

In a large mixing bowl, combine yeast, warm water and sugar. Proof yeast until foamy, about 10 minutes.

Meanwhile, over medium heat, in a small saucepan heat buttermilk, salt and 1 tablespoon butter until warm. Butter need not melt. Set aside and cool to lukewarm.

Add flour, egg, sage and onions, reserving 1/4 cup of onions, to yeast mixture. Mix well.

Knead well on a floured surface until smooth and elastic.

Turn in a greased bowl. Cover and let rise until doubled, about 1 hour. Punch down.

Grease a large baking sheet and dust with cornmeal.

Divide dough into 16 equal parts. Form rolls and place seam down on prepared baking sheet. Cover and let rise for 60 minutes.

Wash rolls with egg. Top each roll with reserved onions. Wash with egg again.

Bake 30 minutes until lightly browned and test done. Turn rolls out on wire rack to cool.

1 large onion, diced
3 tablespoons butter, divided
1 packet active dry yeast
1/4 cup warm water
1 teaspoon sugar
1 cup buttermilk
1 teaspoon salt
4-1/2 cups bread flour
1 egg, beaten
1 teaspoon ground sage
cornmeal for dusting
1 beaten egg for wash

Preheat oven to 375°

PEASANT PISTOU SWIRL LOAF

1 Large Loaf

Bread:

1 cup buttermilk, divided

1/4 cup water

1/4 cup butter

1-1/2 cups all-purpose flour

2 packets active dry yeast

2 tablespoons sugar

1 teaspoon salt

2 to 2-1/2 cups all-purpose flour

cornmeal for dusting

Filling:

2 tablespoons butter

1/2 cup minced onion

2 tablespoons minced fresh parsley

2 tablespoons minced fresh basil

2 cloves minced garlic

1/2 teaspoon salt

1/4 cup freshly grated parmesan cheese

Preheat oven to 350°

Served warm, this is a striking loaf — perfect for a company spaghetti supper. For a special breakfast treat, serve toasted leftovers with scrambled eggs.

In small saucepan, heat 3/4 cup buttermilk, water and butter until lukewarm. The butter need not melt completely. Mixture may curdle. Cool to lukewarm.

In a large bowl, mix 1-1/2 cups flour, yeast, sugar, 1 teaspoon salt, and 1/4 cup room-temperature buttermilk. Proof until yeast is foamy.

Add butter mixture to the yeast mixture. Mix well. Stir in 1-1/2 cups flour to make a sticky dough.

Dust a clean, dry surface with 1/2 cup flour. Turn out dough and knead until flour is absorbed, adding additional flour if necessary. Continue kneading 5 to 10 minutes until dough is smooth and elastic.

Place in buttered bowl, turning once to coat dough. Cover and let rise, about 60 minutes, until doubled.

Meanwhile, prepare filling: melt 2 tablespoons butter in small saucepan. Add onion, parsley, basil, garlic and salt. Turn off burner. Let mixture rest in butter.

Grease a baking sheet and dust with cornmeal.

Punch down dough. Roll out on lightly floured surface to form a 14" x 5" rectangle. Spread filling on dough, leaving a 1" border on all sides. Sprinkle parmesan over filling. Roll dough tightly from the long side, pinching edges to seal. Place seam side down on prepared sheet.

Cover and let rise until doubled, about 30 minutes. Apply wash if desired.

Place a pan of very hot water on the bottom, or bottom shelf of oven. Bake 30 minutes until golden and tests done. Turn out on wire rack to cool.

ROMANO OLIVE BREAD

1 Large Loaf

We like the strong flavors of dry cured black olives and romano cheese. The recipe will work with any type of olives and hard cheese.

In a large bowl, mix 1-1/2 cups flour, yeast, sugar and salt.

In small saucepan, heat buttermilk, water and butter until lukewarm. The butter need not melt completely. Mixture may curdle.

Add lukewarm buttermilk mixture to the yeast mixture. Mix well. Let rest a few minutes until dough smells yeasty. Mix in romano cheese.

Stir in semolina flour and 1 cup bread flour to make a sticky dough.

Dust a clean, dry surface with 1/2 cup bread flour. Turn out dough and knead until flour is absorbed, adding additional flour if necessary. Continue kneading 5 to 10 minutes until dough is smooth and elastic, kneading in olives at end.

Place in buttered bowl, turning once to coat dough. Cover and let rise, about 60 minutes, until doubled.

Grease a baking sheet and dust with cornmeal.

Place bread seam down on prepared baking sheet.

Cover and let rise until doubled, about 45 minutes.

Apply a wash if desired.

Place a pan of very hot water on the bottom, or bottom shelf of oven. Bake 35 minutes until golden and tests done. Turn out on wire rack to cool.

1-1/2 cups bread flour
2 packets active dry yeast
2 tablespoons sugar
1 teaspoon salt
1 cup buttermilk
1/4 cup water
1/4 cup butter
1/2 cup freshly grated romano cheese
1 cup semolina flour
1 to 1-1/2 cups bread flour
1/2 cup diced, pitted, dry-cured black olives
cornmeal for dusting

Preheat oven to 350°

SALTY RYE CARAWAY SANDWICH ROLLS

8 Large Rolls

2 packets active dry
 yeast
pinch of sugar
1 cup lukewarm water
1 cup room-
 temperature
 buttermilk
3 tablespoons kosher
 or coarse salt,
 divided
1/8 cup vegetable oil
5 tablespoons
 caraway seeds,
 divided
1 cup rye flour
1 cup whole wheat
 flour
3-1/2 cups bread flour
cornmeal for dusting
1 well-beaten egg

Preheat oven to 375°

These rolls are perfect for roast beef, ham and cheese or hot pastrami sandwiches. They also make elegant individual dinner loaves.

In a large bowl, dissolve the yeast and sugar in the water. Proof yeast until foamy, about 10 minutes. Add the buttermilk, 1 tablespoon salt, oil and 3 tablespoons caraway seeds and mix well.

Add rye and whole wheat flours. Add 3 cups bread flour, one cup at a time, mixing well after each cup. Knead in remaining bread flour until the dough is no longer sticky.

Continue kneading 5 to 10 minutes until dough is smooth and elastic. Place in buttered bowl, turning once to coat dough. Cover and let rise, about 30 minutes. Dough will not quite double.

Punch down dough. Cut dough into 8 pieces. Knead each piece into smooth ball. Place on floured surface. Cover and let rise 30 minutes.

Grease two baking sheets. Dust with cornmeal.

Shape each ball into a 6" long roll. Place 3" to 4" apart on baking sheets. Cover and let rise 30 minutes.

In a small bowl, mix 2 tablespoons caraway seeds and 2 tablespoons of salt. Brush loaves with beaten egg and sprinkle with salt-seed mixture.

Bake 30 to 35 minutes, until dark golden brown and test done. Turn out on a wire rack to cool.

SAMSON'S BREAD

2 Loaves or 16 Rolls

This is a wonderful, hearty bread with lots of crunch.

In a large bowl, mix the water, yeast and molasses. Proof yeast until foamy, about 10 minutes.

Mix in buttermilk, oil, eggs and salt. Mix in flours, flakes, oats, and seeds to form a soft dough.

Dust a clean, dry surface with white bread flour. Turn out dough and knead, adding more flour if necessary. Continue kneading 5 to 10 minutes until dough is smooth and elastic. Dough will be slightly sticky.

Place in buttered bowl, turning once to coat dough. Cover and let rise, about 60 minutes, until doubled.

Grease a baking sheet and dust with cornmeal.

Divide dough in half. Shape into two round loaves or 16 rolls.

Cover and let rise again until doubled, about 60 minutes.

Apply a wash if desired.

Bake loaves 40 to 45 minutes. Bake rolls 20 to 25 minutes. Bread will be golden brown. Turn out on a wire rack to cool.

1/3 cup lukewarm water

2 packets active dry yeast

2 tablespoons molasses

1 cup room-temperature buttermilk

1/4 cup vegetable oil

2 beaten eggs

1 teaspoon salt

1-1/2 cups whole wheat flour

2 cups white bread flour

1 cup rye flour

1/2 cup soy, barley or rye flakes

1/2 cup quick-cooking oats

1/2 cup salted sunflower seeds

cornmeal for dusting

Preheat oven to 375°

> Soy, barley or rye flakes are available in health food stores. They are similar to oatmeal, but keep their texture when baked and provide an incomparable crunchiness.

TOASTED ONION CHEDDAR BREAD

1 Loaf

1 packet active dry yeast

1/4 cup lukewarm water

1 tablespoon sugar

1 tablespoon dried minced onion

1 cup room-temperature buttermilk

1 teaspoon salt

3 cups bread flour

1 cup grated extra-sharp cheddar cheese

Preheat oven to 375°

This bread has a wonderful aroma while baking. Your mouth will start to water long before the loaf is done.

In a large bowl, dissolve the yeast and sugar in the water. Proof yeast until foamy, about 10 minutes.

In a small, dry skillet, over medium-high heat, shake the dried onion until golden brown, about 1-1/2 minutes. Remove pan from heat.

Add the buttermilk, salt and 1-1/2 cups flour to the yeast mixture. Mix well. Add cheese and toasted onion. Mix well. Mix in remaining flour.

Knead 5 to 10 minutes on lightly floured surface until dough is smooth and elastic.

Place in buttered bowl, turning once to coat dough. Cover and let rise, about 60 minutes, until doubled.

Grease an 8" x 4" loaf pan.

Punch down dough and shape into smooth oblong loaf. Place in prepared pan. Cover and let rise 50 to 60 minutes.

Apply a wash if desired.

Bake 30 to 35 minutes, until dark golden brown and tests done. Turn out on a wire rack to cool.

WHOLE WHEAT OATMEAL BREAD

2 Small Loaves

Hearty and healthy!

In a medium-size mixing bowl, pour boiling water over oats. Mix in honey, butter and salt. Set aside until cool to lukewarm.

In a large mixing bowl, mix yeast, buttermilk and honey. Let proof 10 minutes. Stir in oat mixture and flours.

Knead well on a floured surface until smooth and elastic.

Turn in a greased bowl. Cover and let rise until doubled, about 75 minutes.

Grease a baking sheet and dust with cornmeal.

Punch down dough. Shape into a round loaf. Place on prepared sheet. Cover and let rise until doubled, about 45 minutes.

Apply a wash if desired.

Bake 45 minutes until bread tests done. Turn out on wire rack to cool.

3/4 cup boiling water
1/2 cup rolled oats
1/4 cup honey
2 tablespoons butter
1/2 tablespoon salt
1 packet active dry yeast
1/2 cup room-temperature buttermilk
1 teaspoon honey
1-1/2 cups whole wheat flour
1-1/2 cups bread flour
cornmeal for dusting

Preheat oven to 375°

SWEET BREAD DOUGH

2 Large Loaves or 2 Dozen Sweet Rolls

2 packets active dry yeast

4 tablespoons sugar

1/2 cup lukewarm water

6 cups all-purpose flour

3/4 cup melted butter, cooled to room temperature

1 egg, beaten

2 cups buttermilk

This dough is the basis of our SWEET BREAD DOUGH VARIATIONS that follow.

In a large mixing bowl, mix yeast, sugar and water. Proof yeast about 10 minutes until foamy.

Stir in flour, butter, egg and buttermilk.

Knead well on a floured surface until smooth and elastic.

Turn in a greased bowl to coat dough. Cover and let rise about 1 hour.

Dough may be refrigerated for several days.

See SWEET BREAD DOUGH VARIATIONS.

SWEET CHEESE ROLLS

Sweet Bread Dough Variation #1   About 2 Dozen

8 ounces cream cheese, softened

1/4 cup sugar

3 tablespoons flour

1 egg yolk

grated zest and juice of 1/2 lemon

1/2 batch SWEET BREAD DOUGH

1 egg white for wash

Preheat oven to 375°.

Grease baking sheets.

Beat cream cheese and sugar until light and fluffy. Stir in flour, egg yolk, lemon zest and juice.

Roll SWEET BREAD DOUGH into a 15" square. Cut into 3" squares. Place on prepared baking sheets.

Place about 1 tablespoon cheese mixture in center of each square. Bring 2 diagonally opposite corners to center of each square, overlapping slightly. Pinch to seal. Let rise until double, about 30 minutes. Brush with egg white.

Bake 12 to 15 minutes until golden.

Top with icing, if desired.

CINNAMON ROLLS

12 to 14 Buns **Sweet Bread Dough Variation #2**

Roll dough into 8" x 15" rectangle. Brush with melted butter leaving 1/2" border. Sprinkle with sugar and cinnamon, then raisins and/or nuts. Roll tightly from long side. Pinch ends to seal. Slice roll with a sharp knife into 1" thick slices, cutting slowly to avoid squashing dough. Place in greased 9" cake pans, with sides nearly touching.

Cover. Let rise 35 to 45 minutes, until nearly doubled.

Bake 25 minutes. Cool slightly and glaze with any FRUIT ICING.

1/2 batch SWEET BREAD DOUGH

1 tablespoon melted butter

1/2 cup brown sugar

cinnamon for sprinkling (about 2 teaspoons)

1/2 cup raisins and/or walnuts

Preheat oven to 375°

STICKY BUNS

12 to 14 Buns **Sweet Bread Dough Variation #3**

Prepare rolls using CINNAMON ROLLS recipe through slicing step, substituting pecans for raisins.

Grease muffin cups.

In the bottom of each muffin cup, place 1 teaspoon melted butter and 1 teaspoon warmed honey. Cover honey with 1 tablespoon brown sugar. Place cut rolls, cut side down on top of mixture in each cup.

Cover and let rise 35 to 45 minutes, until nearly doubled.

Bake for 30 minutes until golden brown. Turn out warm rolls.

1/2 batch SWEET BREAD DOUGH

1/2 cup pecans

4 tablespoons butter, melted

4 tablespoons warmed honey

3/4 cup dark brown sugar

Preheat oven to 400°

MARZIPAN SWIRL LOAF

Sweet Bread Dough Variation #4

1/2 batch SWEET BREAD DOUGH

7 ounces almond paste

1/4 cup sugar

1 egg, separated

1/4 cup slivered almonds

1/4 cup dried cherries, chopped (optional)

Preheat oven to 375°

A sophisticated twist. Makes sublime toast.

Grease a baking sheet. On a lightly floured surface, roll dough into a 9" x 18" rectangle.

Beat together almond paste, sugar and egg white until smooth. Spread it on the dough leaving a 1/2" border. Sprinkle with almonds and cherries.

Roll tightly from the short side. Tuck ends. Place on prepared sheet. Cover and let rise 35 to 45 minutes, until nearly doubled. Wash with egg yolk beaten with teaspoon of water.

Bake 35 to 40 minutes until tests done. Turn out on wire rack to cool.

Prepared almond paste is sold commercially in cans or tubes. Although it is a trifle expensive, it is packed with flavor and has a long shelf life. Store opened paste in the refrigerator or freezer. Don't confuse almond paste with prepared marzipan, which is basically almond paste with more sugar.

Use leftover almond paste in just about any bread, cake, cookie or muffin dough as a great flavor enhancer.

A World of Pizzas

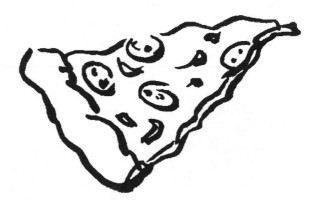

ABOUT PIZZAS

Pizzas made at home cost about a third of the ones delivered to your door and they're always hot. No tipping, please.

We think the best part of homemade pizza is the freedom cooks have to top them with just about anything. Pizza provides a tasty base for small bits of leftover meats, cheeses and vegetables.

Pizza crusts are available commercially in a variety of forms, but we think you'll get hooked on making our BASIC PIZZA CRUST DOUGH. Just remember to start it about an hour before you want to eat or make it ahead and store it in the refrigerator. Pizza sauce is also easily made and can be seasoned to match your personal preferences. Make a large batch and store it in usable portions in the freezer.

Pizza dough is sometimes reluctant to spread and stretch. If your dough keeps snapping back, cover it with a towel and let it rest a few minutes to allow the gluten in the dough to relax. Continue shaping it to desired size. If you want to try hand tossing, catch it on your wrists, not your fingertips, turning and stretching the pizza dough to desired shape and size while tossing it up just a few inches.

Pizzas cook best on a baking stone or unglazed tiles. Dust the stone with cornmeal and then prepare the pizza right on the stone. For an even crisper crust, place the stone in the oven before you preheat it so that it will be hot when you're ready to bake your pizza. Don't dust it with cornmeal until you're ready to add the pizza, which you have prepared on a cornmeal dusted peel (flat wooden or metal paddle). Tip the peel toward the stone and quickly jerk the peel out, leaving the pizza on the stone.

Take care not to grease your baking stone or wash it with soap, just sweep off any burned crumbs. If you must rinse the stone, make sure it has dried completely before heating it or it may crack. You can, however, leave your baking stone in the oven during the self-cleaning cycle and dust off any resulting ash.

Rectangular pizzas cut into small squares are popular party appetizers.

BASIC PIZZA CRUST DOUGH

12" Round or Square Pizza

This recipe makes an excellent, classically thin pizza. The buttermilk lends a slight sourdough flavor to the crust.

In a large mixing bowl, mix yeast, water, oil and honey. Proof yeast until foamy, about 10 minutes.

Mix in flour, salt and buttermilk and form into a ball. Add water, 1 tablespoon at a time if dough is dry.

Knead dough on a lightly floured surface until smooth and elastic, about 7 minutes. Turn dough in an olive-oiled bowl. Cover and let rise until doubled, about 45 minutes.

Dust a stone baking tile or greased baking sheet with cornmeal. Spread (or test your tossing skills — you can do it!) dough to form a 12" square or circle. Turn up edges to form a thicker rim.

Add traditional toppings or try some of the more exotic pizzas in this chapter.

1 packet active dry yeast

1/3 cup lukewarm water

1 tablespoon olive oil

1 teaspoon honey or sugar

2-1/2 cups all-purpose flour

1/2 teaspoon salt

1/2 cup buttermilk at room temperature

1 to 3 tablespoons water

cornmeal for dusting

Preheat oven to 375°

WHOLE WHEAT PIZZA CRUST DOUGH:

Substitute an equal amount of whole wheat flour for any or all of the all-purpose flour.

GARLIC and HERB PIZZA CRUST DOUGH:

Add 1-1/2 teaspoon dried basil, oregano or rosemary and 1 large clove very finely minced garlic to yeast mixture after it has proofed.

CORNMEAL or SEMOLINA PIZZA CRUST DOUGH:

Replace 1/2 cup flour with 1/2 cup cornmeal or semolina flour.

CHEESE PIZZA CRUST DOUGH:

Add 1/2 cup grated parmesan cheese to dry ingredients.

HOMEMADE PIZZA SAUCE

About 4 Cups

1 tablespoon olive oil

1/2 cup minced onion

2 cloves crushed garlic

28-ounce can crushed plum tomatoes

1/2 teaspoon salt

1/4 teaspoon pepper

1 teaspoon sugar

1/2 teaspoon dried oregano

2 teaspoons chopped fresh basil

1/4 teaspoon dried red pepper flakes or to taste

Yes, you can buy it. But it's better when you season it to suit your own taste.

Heat olive oil over medium heat. Sauté onion a few minutes until softened but not browned. Add garlic and sauté 1 minute more. Add tomatoes, salt, pepper, sugar, oregano, basil and red pepper. Simmer 20 minutes to thicken slightly.

For an even stronger tomato flavor, stir 2 or 3 tablespoons of tomato paste into the sauce before simmering.

Unused portions may be refrigerated a few days or frozen.

"ALL-AMERICAN" PIZZA

12" Pizza

1 recipe BASIC PIZZA CRUST DOUGH

1 cup HOMEMADE PIZZA SAUCE

any number of America's Favorite Toppings

1 cup shredded extra-sharp cheddar cheese

1-1/2 cups shredded mozzarella cheese

extra-virgin olive oil

Prepare BASIC PIZZA CRUST DOUGH.

Spread sauce on dough, leaving edges plain. Spread with any number of America's Favorite Toppings (see below). Sprinkle evenly with cheese. Drizzle with a very small amount of extra-virgin olive oil. Bake 20 to 25 minutes until crust is slightly browned.

America's Favorite Toppings: pepperoni; bell peppers; mushrooms; onions; chopped meatballs or Italian sausages; olives; raw shrimp; cooked chicken or pork.

Preheat oven to 375°

ARTICHOKE AND OLIVE PIZZA

Prepare BASIC PIZZA CRUST DOUGH.

Drain and quarter artichokes.

Spread HOMEMADE PIZZA SAUCE on dough, leaving edges plain. Distribute artichokes, olives and onion evenly over pizza.

Mix cheeses and sprinkle over pizza. Drizzle with a very small amount of extra-virgin olive oil.

Bake 20 to 25 minutes until crust is lightly browned.

1 recipe BASIC PIZZA CRUST DOUGH

12-ounce jar marinated artichoke hearts

1 cup HOMEMADE PIZZA SAUCE

1/2 cup pitted, coarsely chopped kalamata or other black olives

1 small, sliced, sautéed onion (optional)

1-1/2 cups grated jarlsberg, emmenthaler or gruyere cheese

1-1/2 cups grated extra sharp cheddar cheese

extra-virgin olive oil

Preheat oven to 375°

BACON and BRIE PIZZA

12" Pizza

1 recipe BASIC
PIZZA CRUST
DOUGH

6 slices bacon

6 ounces chilled brie
cheese, coarsely
chopped

1/2 teaspoon dried
oregano

4 ounces shredded
muenster cheese

dried red pepper
flakes (optional)

extra-virgin olive oil

Prepare BASIC PIZZA CRUST DOUGH.

Cook bacon until done but not crisp. Drain well.

Dice bacon and sprinkle over crust. Add brie. Sprinkle with dried oregano. Cover with muenster cheese. Sprinkle with dried red pepper flakes to taste. Drizzle with a very small amount of extra-virgin olive oil.

Bake 20 to 25 minutes until crust is lightly browned.

Preheat oven to 375°

BARBECUE PIZZA

Use your own favorite homemade or commercial barbecue sauce in this recipe.

Prepare CORNMEAL PIZZA CRUST DOUGH.

While dough is rising, sauté sausage in a skillet until browned, breaking into small chunks with a fork. Drain off fat and then blot meat with paper towels.

Mix meat with barbecue sauce and red pepper flakes, if desired. Spread sauce over crust. Sprinkle evenly with cheeses. Drizzle with a very small amount of extra-virgin olive oil.

Bake 20 to 25 minutes until crust is lightly browned.

1 recipe CORNMEAL PIZZA CRUST DOUGH

12- to 16-ounce log spicy bulk pork breakfast sausage

1 cup tomato-based barbecue sauce

1/4 teaspoon dried red pepper flakes (optional)

1/2 pound shredded smoked cheddar or gouda cheese

1/4 pound shredded mozzarella cheese

extra-virgin olive oil

Preheat oven to 375°

BROCCOLI PIZZA

12" Pizza

1 recipe WHOLE
   WHEAT PIZZA
   CRUST DOUGH
1 cup HOMEMADE
   PIZZA SAUCE
1 cup small broccoli
   florets
1/2 cup finely diced
   onion
dried red pepper
   flakes (optional)
1-1/2 cups shredded
   mozzarella or
   fontina cheese
extra-virgin olive oil

Preheat oven to 375°

Prepare WHOLE WHEAT PIZZA CRUST DOUGH.

Spread with pizza sauce. Distribute broccoli florets and onion over sauce. Sprinkle with dried red pepper flakes if desired. Sprinkle with cheese. Drizzle with a very small amount of extra-virgin olive oil.

Bake 20 to 25 minutes until crust is lightly browned.

CARAMELIZED ONION, WILD MUSHROOM and STILTON PIZZA

12" Pizza

Prepare BASIC PIZZA CRUST DOUGH.

Heat 2 tablespoons olive oil in a large skillet over medium heat. Add onion. Sauté, stirring occasionally, 5 to 10 minutes until onion has softened slightly. Reduce heat to low. Cover and cook onion, stirring occasionally, until golden brown but not burned.

At the same time, in another skillet, sauté mushrooms in 2 teaspoons olive oil until softened, 5 to 10 minutes. Set aside.

Spread onions evenly on prepared crust. Distribute mushrooms over pizza. Crumble cheese over top. Drizzle with a very small amount of extra-virgin olive oil.

Bake 20 to 25 minutes until crust is lightly browned.

1 recipe BASIC PIZZA CRUST DOUGH

2 tablespoons extra-virgin olive oil

2 large Spanish onions, thinly sliced (about 2 pounds)

2 teaspoons extra-virgin olive oil

1 cup sliced portobello, shiitake or button mushrooms

4 ounces stilton or other mild blue cheese

extra-virgin olive oil

Preheat oven to 375°

CHINESE PIZZA

12" Pizza

1 recipe BASIC
  PIZZA CRUST
  DOUGH, modified
  as directed

1/3 to 1/2 pound
  lapschong (sweet
  Chinese pork
  sausage)

1/2 cup hoisin sauce

2 to 3 chopped
  scallions

julienned bamboo
  slices (optional)

oriental dark sesame
  oil

Prepare BASIC PIZZA CRUST DOUGH, substituting oriental dark sesame oil for the olive oil.

Steam sausages for 15 to 20 minutes until softened. When sausage is cool enough to handle, slice it in thin diagonal slices. Spread crust with hoisin sauce. Distribute sausages evenly over sauce. Sprinkle with scallions. Add several bamboo shoots if desired. Drizzle with a very small amount of additional sesame oil.

Bake 20 to 25 minutes until crust is lightly browned.

Preheat oven to 375°

GREEK PIZZA

12" Pizza

Prepare GARLIC and HERB PIZZA DOUGH.

Cover with a layer of sliced tomatoes. Sprinkle with oregano and kasseri cheese. Add pepperocini if desired. Cover with feta cheese. Drizzle with a very small amount of extra-virgin olive oil.

Bake 20 to 25 minutes until crust is lightly browned.

1 recipe GARLIC and HERB PIZZA CRUST DOUGH using oregano

3 or 4 fresh, ripe red tomatoes, thinly sliced

1/2 teaspoon dried oregano

1/4 cup freshly grated kasseri or romano cheese

1/4 cup chopped pepperocini (mild pickled peppers) (optional)

6 ounces feta cheese, crumbled

extra-virgin olive oil

Preheat oven to 375°

HONOLULU PIZZA

12" Pizza

1 recipe BASIC or
  WHOLE WHEAT
  PIZZA CRUST
  DOUGH
1 cup HOMEMADE
  PIZZA SAUCE
20 ounce can
  pineapple chunks,
  well drained
3/4 cup finely diced
  baked ham or
  Canadian bacon
1-1/2 cups shredded
  mozzarella cheese

Prepare BASIC or WHOLE WHEAT PIZZA CRUST DOUGH.

Spread with pizza sauce. Pat pineapple chunks dry with paper towels. Distribute over crust. Add ham. Sprinkle with mozzarella.

Bake 20 to 25 minutes until crust is lightly browned.

Preheat oven to 375°

PESTO PIZZA

12" Pizza

1 recipe BASIC
  PIZZA CRUST
  DOUGH
1 cup PESTO SAUCE
1/2 cup drained oil-
  packed sun-dried
  tomatoes, finely
  chopped
3/4 cup freshly shaved
  parmesan cheese

See our recipe for PESTO SAUCE or use one commercially prepared. The easiest way to shave parmesan is to use a swivel vegetable peeler and a well-chilled block of cheese.

Prepare BASIC PIZZA CRUST DOUGH.

Spread with PESTO SAUCE. Sprinkle with sun-dried tomatoes and parmesan cheese.

Bake 20 to 25 minutes until crust is lightly browned.

Preheat oven to 375°

ROQUEFORT, WALNUT and RED ONION PIZZA

Prepare BASIC PIZZA CRUST DOUGH.

Heat 1 tablespoon olive oil in a skillet over medium heat. Saute onion until softened but not browned, about 5 minutes. Add garlic, salt and pepper. Remove from heat and stir in walnuts. Spread mixture on crust. Sprinkle with roquefort and cheddar cheeses. Drizzle with a very small amount of extra-virgin olive oil.

Bake 20 to 25 minutes until crust is lightly browned.

1 recipe BASIC PIZZA CRUST DOUGH

1 tablespoon extra-virgin olive oil

1 large sliced red onion (about 1 pound)

1 to 2 cloves minced garlic

1/4 teaspoon salt

1/4 teaspoon freshly ground pepper

1/2 cup chopped walnuts

2 to 3 ounces crumbled roquefort or other blue cheese

1 cup shredded mild cheddar cheese

extra-virgin olive oil

Preheat oven to 375°

SOUTH OF THE BORDER PIZZA

12" Pizza

1 recipe CORNMEAL
  PIZZA CRUST
  DOUGH

1/2 cup chopped onion

1 tablespoon extra-
  virgin olive oil

1 clove minced garlic

1-1/2 cups cooked
  pinto or black beans

1/4 cup water

1/2 teaspoon ground
  cumin

1/2 teaspoon salt

1/2 cup salsa

2 tablespoons
  chopped fresh
  cilantro or parsley

1 or more chopped
  jalapeño peppers or
  other hot chili
  peppers, seeded if
  desired

3/4 cup shredded
  monterey jack
  cheese

3/4 cup shredded
  mozzarella cheese

1/4 teaspoon dried
  oregano

extra-virgin olive oil

Prepare CORNMEAL PIZZA CRUST
DOUGH.

Saute chopped onion in 1 tablespoon olive oil
until softened but not browned. Add garlic
and cook 1 minute. Stir in beans, water,
cumin and salt. Simmer over medium heat
until most of liquid has evaporated, pressing
beans against the side of the pan to mash.
Continue mashing until beans reach desired
consistency.

Spread beans on crust. Cover beans with
salsa. Sprinkle with cilantro. Add jalapeño
pepper. Sprinkle with cheeses. Sprinkle with
oregano. Drizzle with a very small amount of
extra-virgin olive oil.

Bake 20 to 25 minutes until crust is lightly
browned.

Preheat oven to 375°

SPINACH RICOTTA PIZZA
with ROASTED RED PEPPERS

12" Pizza

Prepare BASIC PIZZA CRUST DOUGH.

Blanch fresh spinach in boiling water until wilted. Drain and squeeze out all excess liquid. Spread evenly on prepared pizza crust. Distribute red pepper evenly over spinach. Drop ricotta cheese in small mounds over pepper. Sprinkle pizza evenly with mozzarella. Drizzle with a very small amount of extra-virgin olive oil.

Bake 20 to 25 minutes until crust is lightly browned.

1 recipe BASIC PIZZA CRUST DOUGH

2 pounds fresh spinach, trimmed and washed well or 20 ounces frozen chopped spinach, thawed and squeezed dry

1 red bell pepper, roasted, peeled and seeded or an equivalent amount of jarred roasted red pepper

1 cup ricotta cheese

1-1/2 cups shredded mozzarella cheese

extra-virgin olive oil

Preheat oven to 375°

WHITE GARLIC PIZZA

12" Pizza

**1 recipe BASIC or
GARLIC and HERB
PIZZA CRUST
DOUGH**

**1/4 cup extra-virgin
olive oil**

**2 cloves crushed or
minced garlic**

**1/4 teaspoon dried
oregano**

**2 cups shredded
mozzarella cheese**

Preheat oven to 375°

*If you leave the garlic in the oil, it may burn
and leave a bitter taste.*

Prepare BASIC or GARLIC and HERB
PIZZA CRUST DOUGH.

While dough is rising, pour olive oil into a
small skillet or saucepan. Add garlic and heat
oil over very low heat 10 minutes. Do not
allow garlic to brown. Strain oil, discard
garlic, and set aside.

After forming pizza, brush with garlic oil,
reserving a small amount. Sprinkle pizza with
oregano. Spread cheese evenly over pizza.
Drizzle with reserved garlic oil.

Bake 20 to 25 minutes until crust is lightly
browned.

Appetizers,
Beverages,
Snacks &
Spreads

CAJUN SHRIMP DIP

Adjust the amount of hot pepper and oriental chili sauce to suit your palate. Compliments on this dip usually increase with the amount of "heat" used.

Puree cottage cheese, buttermilk and lemon juice in blender or food processor until smooth. Stir in onion, horseradish, Worcestershire sauce, hot pepper sauce, oriental chili sauce, catsup, chili sauce, sugar, salt and shrimp.

> Oriental hot chili sauce with garlic is available at Asian import stores and most supermarkets.

3/4 cup cottage cheese

1/4 cup buttermilk

2 tablespoons fresh lemon juice

6 tablespoons finely minced onion

2-1/2 tablespoons prepared horseradish

1 teaspoon Worcestershire sauce

1 teaspoon hot pepper sauce

2 teaspoons oriental hot chili sauce with garlic

1/2 cup catsup

1/2 cup bottled chili sauce

1 tablespoon sugar

1 teaspoon salt

3 cups cleaned, cooked, finely diced shrimp

Appetizers, Beverages, Snacks & Spreads

CARAWAY CHEESE COINS

9 to 10 Dozen Crackers

1 cup softened butter

2 cups buttermilk

12 ounces grated sharp cheddar cheese

2 tablespoons caraway or cumin seeds

4 cups all-purpose flour

Preheat oven to 350°

The dough for these flavorful crackers freezes well, making this a great "have-on-hand" company snack. The crackers are wonderful plain or serve as a great base for all your favorite spreads.

Cream butter. Beat in buttermilk, cheese and caraway seeds. Beat in flour.

Shape into two loaves about 2" in diameter. Wrap the rolls in wax paper.

Chill at least 6 hours up to 4 days, or store in freezer up to 2 months.

To serve, slice off desired amount in 1/4" thick slices. Place 2" apart on greased baking sheets. Return unused portion to refrigerator.

Bake 20 to 25 minutes until golden. Serve hot or at room temperature.

KIELBASA SAUERKRAUT RYE LOAF

1 Loaf

This recipe is dedicated to Bert Gould and his mother, Mimi. Mimi is a mother of three, grandmother of 21, and great-grandmother of 25. On Easter morning, Mimi cooks kielbasa for the whole gang.

In a large mixing bowl, combine yeast, water and pinch of sugar. Let proof until foamy, about 10 minutes.

Meanwhile, in a heavy saucepan heat buttermilk, butter, sugar and salt until just warmed.

Beat warmed mixture and egg into proofed yeast, mixing well. Stir in sauerkraut and flours. Knead about 10 minutes until dough is smooth and elastic.

Place in a greased bowl, turning once to coat. Cover and let rise about 1 hour until doubled.

Punch down. Pat out to form a rectangle long enough to hold the the kielbasa with 1" or so border at the ends. Form a loaf by enveloping the kielbasa and turning under the ends. Place seam down on greased baking sheet sprinkled with cornmeal. Cover and let rise 45 minutes to 1 hour until nearly doubled.

Apply a wash or dust with white flour for a rustic look, if desired.

Bake 35 to 40 minutes until loaf tests done.

1 packet active dry yeast
1/4 cup warm water
pinch of sugar
1/2 cup buttermilk
2 tablespoons butter
1 tablespoon sugar
1 teaspoon salt
1 egg
1 cup rinsed, squeezed-dry, chopped sauerkraut
2 cups rye flour
1-1/4 to 1-1/2 cups all-purpose flour
1 kielbasa sausage, about 8" long (half a kielbasa ring)
cornmeal for dusting

Preheat oven to 400°

> For more information about working with yeast breads, read the introduction to the YEAST BREADS chapter.

NEW AGE PIMENTO CHEESE SPREAD

1 Pound

1 pound extra-sharp cheddar cheese, diced

1 roasted red pepper (or 2/3 of 7-ounce jar)

2 tablespoons sugar

1/3 cup buttermilk

A versatile recipe which serves as a spread for crackers, a dip for vegetables, a terrific celery stuffer or a sandwich filling.

Process all ingredients in a food processor until smooth.

Chilling this spread for several hours enhances its flavor.

NEW DELHI CURRY DIP

Makes 1-3/4 Cups

1 cup cottage cheese

1/2 cup buttermilk

1 clove garlic, crushed

1 teaspoon minced gingerroot

1 teaspoon curry powder

1/2 teaspoon ground cumin

1/2 teaspoon ground coriander

1 teaspoon sugar

8-ounce (small) can crushed pineapple, well drained

3 tablespoons flaked coconut

Puree cottage cheese, buttermilk, garlic and gingerroot in blender or food processor until smooth.

Stir in curry powder, cumin, coriander, sugar, pineapple and coconut.

Chill at least 2 hours to blend flavors.

Serve with crackers, chips or vegetables.

NON-KOSHER CHOPPED CHICKEN LIVER

About 1-1/2 Pounds

Soaking the liver in buttermilk removes any traces of bitterness from the liver in this traditional spread. Try to use the chicken fat. It gives a much better flavor!

1 pound chicken livers

1/2 cup or more buttermilk

4 tablespoons rendered chicken fat or butter

3 cups chopped onion

2 hard cooked eggs, peeled

1 teaspoon salt

freshly ground pepper (optional)

chopped parsley

additional chopped raw onion and hard boiled egg for garnish

Cut livers in half, discarding membranes. Soak overnight in buttermilk to cover. Drain and rinse briefly under running water. Set aside.

Heat chicken fat in a large skillet. Add chopped onion and cook until softened, 5 minutes or more. Add liver. Cook, stirring frequently, until liver is mostly cooked through — cut one open to check. Cool mixture slightly.

Place liver mixture in food processor with eggs, salt and pepper (in batches, if necessary). Pulse briefly to chop, taking care to maintain a chunky texture. Chill until serving time.

Mound on large serving plate. Sprinkle with parsley and surround with chopped onion and chopped hard cooked egg. Serve with crackers, cocktail dark breads, toast or bagel chips.

How to render chicken fat: Remove any visible hunks of yellow fat and loose skin from a roasting chicken. Cut fat into 1" dice. Place in a saucepan and barely cover with water. Simmer on low heat for 1 hour or more until the fat turns to a clear yellow liquid with tiny floating crisp pieces. Strain. Rendered fat can be stored indefinitely in the refrigerator and is a tasty substitute for butter or shortening in many recipes.

SPINACH SQUARES

About 35 Hors d'Oeuvres

4 tablespoons butter

3 eggs, beaten

1 cup all-purpose
  flour

1 teaspoon salt

1 teaspoon baking
  powder

1/2 teaspoon baking
  soda

1 cup buttermilk

1 pound extra-sharp
  cheddar cheese,
  grated

1/2 cup finely minced
  onion

20 ounces frozen
  chopped spinach,
  thawed, drained and
  squeezed dry

Preheat oven to 350°

Our buttermilk version of Greek spanikopita. Serve these warm and watch them disappear. You can refrigerate and reheat leftovers, if there are any.

Place butter in a 9" x 13" baking pan. Set in preheating oven to melt, taking care not to brown butter. Remove from oven and set aside.

Beat eggs with flour, salt, baking powder and baking soda. Stir in buttermilk. Stir in cheese, onion and spinach.

Swirl melted butter in baking pan to coat. Add spinach mixture.

Bake 35 minutes until center tests done. Cool 10 minutes. Cut in small squares. Serve warm or at room temperature.

Substitute chopped broccoli for the spinach, if desired.

SPRINGTIME IN SIBERIA RADISH DIP

About 2-1/2 Cups

Have fun with this dip. We sometimes add more buttermilk and use it for a salad dressing, or decrease the amount of buttermilk and use it as a spread on bagels or pita bread.

Process cream cheese with buttermilk in food processor until smooth. Stir in pepper. Fold in radishes and scallions. Chill at least 1 hour to blend flavors.

Serve with crackers or vegetables.

8 ounces softened cream cheese

1/2 cup buttermilk

1/2 teaspoon freshly ground pepper

16 ounces red radishes, chopped

8 to 10 scallions, chopped

BUTTERMILK PINKSTER

About 1 Cup

1/2 cup cold tomato
  juice
1/2 cup cold
  buttermilk
1/2 teaspoon lemon
  juice
1 teaspoon prepared
  horseradish

Mix all ingredients well.

PINEAPPLE BUTTERMILK SHAKE

About 2-1/2 Cups

1 cup buttermilk
1 cup fresh or drained
  canned pineapple
  pieces
1 tablespoon sugar
1 ripe banana, in
  chunks

Combine all ingredients in a blender until
smooth.

SIMPLE STRAWBERRY MILKSHAKE

About 2 Cups

3/4 cup buttermilk
10-ounce package
  frozen, unthawed,
  sweetened
  strawberries
1 teaspoon vanilla
  extract
dash salt

Combine all ingredients in a blender until
smooth.

ORANGE BUTTERMILK SMOOTHIE

About 2 Cups

Combine all ingredients in a blender until smooth. For an ORANGE-PINEAPPLE BUTTERMILK SMOOTHIE, add 1/2 cup fresh or drained canned pineapple pieces before blending.

1 cup buttermilk
1/2 cup fresh orange juice
1/2 cup vanilla ice cream
2 tablespoons dark brown sugar

SPARKLING ORANGE PUNCH

About 2 Quarts

Mix buttermilk and 2 cups sherbet in a blender until smooth. Store in refrigerator until serving time. Pour into small punch bowl. Add ginger ale and 1 cup sherbet in small scoops. Add ice cubes if desired.

4 cups buttermilk
3 cups orange sherbet, divided
1 cup ginger ale
orange juice ice cubes (optional)

SPICY PEACH COOLER

About 1 Quart

Combine peaches, brown sugar and cinnamon in a blender until smooth. Stir peach mixture into buttermilk. Chill to allow flavors to blend.

10-ounce package frozen peaches
1/4 cup dark brown sugar
1/2 teaspoon cinnamon
4 cups buttermilk

Main Dishes

BAKED MAPLE PECAN CHICKEN

A favorite pot luck supper dish.

Mix buttermilk and hot pepper sauce in a sealable plastic bag or bowl. Add chicken, coating well. Marinate chicken at least 30 minutes, or more if possible, in refrigerator.

Grind pecans in food processor until finely ground but not pasty.

Mix pecans well with flour, salt and pepper.

Remove chicken from marinade, allowing excess buttermilk to drip off. Coat with pecan mixture.

Place skin side up in large, lightly greased pan.

Mix melted butter with syrup. Drizzle over top of chicken as evenly as possible.

Bake 45 to 55 minutes, until crisp and brown. Best served hot or reheated.

2 cups buttermilk

1/4 to 1/2 teaspoon hot pepper sauce

5 pounds chicken pieces

6 ounces pecan pieces

1-1/4 cups all-purpose flour

1 teaspoon salt

1/4 teaspoon freshly ground pepper

3 tablespoons butter, melted

2 tablespoons real maple syrup

Preheat oven to 350°

BUTTERMILK MEATLOAF

6 to 8 Servings

Meatloaf:
2/3 cup dry bread
crumbs
1 cup buttermilk
1/2 teaspoon dried
thyme
1/4 teaspoon dried
oregano
2 eggs, beaten
2 teaspoons
Worcestershire
sauce
1 teaspoon salt
1/2 teaspoon freshly
ground pepper
1 pound ground beef
1/2 pound bulk
breakfast sausage or
ground pork
1/4 cup minced onion
1 small carrot, grated

Sauce (optional):
3 tablespoons brown
sugar
1/4 cup catsup
1 tablespoon dijon-
style mustard

Preheat oven to 350°

Cold meatloaf makes the best sandwiches!

Grease a 9" x 13" baking pan.

Soak crumbs in buttermilk 5 minutes. Stir in thyme, oregano and eggs, Worcestershire sauce, salt and pepper. Add meats, onion and carrot. Mix well. Shape into loaf and place in prepared pan. Flatten top. (For a less crispy crust, pack into a greased loaf pan.) Mix brown sugar, catsup and mustard. Pour half of sauce over meat loaf. Bake 30 minutes. Brush with remaining sauce. Bake 30 additional minutes. Remove from oven. Let rest 10 minutes before slicing.

More mixing and tighter packing when shaping makes a denser, more terrine-like meatloaf.

CAJUN FRIED CHICKEN

This chicken bites back.

Mix buttermilk and pepper sauce in a sealable plastic bag. Add chicken. Marinate at least 30 minutes in refrigerator.

In another bag, combine flour, pepper, poultry seasoning, cayenne pepper, mustard, garlic powder and salt.

Line a large pan with foil or wax paper. Remove chicken from buttermilk mixture and toss in flour mixture to coat completely. Place on prepared pan and let sit about 15 minutes.

Using a large, deep pan, fry chicken in 1" hot oil until mahogany brown on all sides. Drain on absorbent paper. Serve hot, cold or at room temperature.

2 cups buttermilk

8 drops or more hot pepper sauce

3 pounds chicken pieces

1 cup all-purpose flour

1/2 teaspoon coarsely ground black pepper

3/4 teaspoon poultry seasoning

1/2 teaspoon cayenne pepper or to taste

1/2 teaspoon dry mustard

1 teaspoon garlic powder

1 teaspoon salt

oil for frying

Preheat oil to 370°

CHILI and CORNBREAD CASSEROLE

10 to 12 Servings

Chili:

1 pound hot Italian sausage or ground beef

1 teaspoon olive oil

3 cups chopped onion

2 cloves minced garlic

4 tablespoons hot chili powder

1 teaspoon ground cumin

3/4 teaspoon ground coriander

1 teaspoon dried oregano

12 ounces dark beer

28-ounce can concentrated crushed tomatoes

1/4 teaspoon cayenne pepper

1/2 cup sugar

2 bay leaves

2 tablespoons Worcestershire sauce

2 chipotles (smoked, dried jalapeño chili peppers)

3 cups cooked kidney or pinto beans

Cornbread:

1 cup all-purpose flour

1 cup cornmeal

2 teaspoons baking powder

1 teaspoon baking soda

2 tablespoons sugar or honey

1 cup buttermilk

1 egg, beaten

3 tablespoons melted butter

Preheat oven to 425°

The chili in this recipe was inspired by the Thai fondness for sweet and hot flavors. Chipotles add a subtle smokiness. Most supermarkets carry them these days.

Chili:

Remove casings from sausage if necessary. Coat bottom of large saucepan with olive oil. Brown meat, breaking up with a fork. Add onion and cook 5 to 10 minutes until softened. Add garlic. Cook 1 minute, stirring to distribute garlic. Add chili powder, cumin, coriander and oregano. Stir 1 to 2 minutes until spices are fragrant. Add beer. Bring to a boil. Simmer 5 minutes to reduce slightly. Add tomatoes, cayenne, sugar, bay leaves and Worcestershire sauce. Slit chipotles on one side and add with beans. Stir to mix well. Simmer 35 minutes or longer to blend flavors. If time permits, refrigerate chili overnight and reheat. Remove chipotles and bay leaves and discard. Pour chili into 10" x 14" baking pan.

Cornbread:

Mix flour, cornmeal, baking powder, and baking soda. Stir in sugar. Mix buttermilk, egg and butter. Stir into dry ingredients. Mix well and pour carefully over chili. Bake 20 minutes until topping is firm and beginning to brown.

GREEN AND GOLD RICE CASSEROLE

4 to 6 Servings

This is an excellent one-dish vegetarian dinner, complete with protein, vegetables and a starch. It also makes good use of leftovers. Substitute brussels sprouts, broccoli, kale, chard or other green vegetables for the spinach.

In a medium-size saucepan, over medium heat, bring rice and water to boil. Cover and reduce heat to low. Cook about 15 minutes until rice is done. Set aside.

Melt butter in skillet. Sauté onion until softened but not browned. Add frozen spinach. Cook on medium low, stirring frequently, until the liquid from the spinach is evaporated. Stir in walnuts. Cook 1 minute. Stir in rice. Remove from heat.

In a large mixing bowl, beat eggs with buttermilk. Add salt, pepper and 6 ounces of cheese. Mix well. Stir in rice mixture. Mix well. The mixture will appear dry.

Turn into a buttered 1-1/2 to 2 quart casserole dish. Sprinkle with additional cheese.

Bake about 40 minutes, until heated through and cheese is melted.

1 cup uncooked white rice (or 2 cups cooked leftover rice)

2 cups water

2 tablespoons butter

1/2 cup finely chopped onion

10-ounce package of frozen, chopped, spinach

1/4 cup chopped walnuts

2 eggs

1 cup buttermilk

1 teaspoon salt

1/2 teaspoon freshly ground black pepper

6 ounces extra sharp cheddar cheese (yellow if available), grated

1/4 cup additional, grated cheddar for top

Preheat oven to 350°

MODERN MACARONI and CHEESE

6 Servings

2 cups elbow
  macaroni or other
  pasta
1 tablespoon butter
1/3 cup chopped onion
2/3 cup (about 1 small
  cap) portobello
  mushroom, chopped
2 cups buttermilk
2 beaten eggs
6 ounces swiss cheese,
  grated
1/2 teaspoon
  Worcestershire
  sauce
1/8 teaspoon cayenne
  pepper
1-1/2 teaspoons salt
Additional grated
  swiss cheese

Preheat oven to 350°

The same idea, but a totally different taste.

Cook macaroni 2 minutes less than package directions suggest. Drain and set aside.

While the macaroni is cooking, melt the butter in a small skillet and sauté onion and mushroom until mushroom darkens, about 5 minutes.

In a medium bowl, mix buttermilk, eggs, cheese, Worcestershire sauce, cayenne pepper and salt. Stir in mushroom mixture. Add the macaroni and stir to coat.

Turn into a greased 9" square baking pan. Sprinkle with additional cheese. Bake 45 minutes until crusty and golden.

MUSHROOM QUICHE

In a medium-size skillet, sauté onions and mushrooms in butter until mushrooms are slightly browned.

Meanwhile, place prepared pie crust in a 10" quiche pan or a 9" pie plate. Prick bottom all over with a fork. Pre-bake pie crust for 10 minutes. Remove from oven.

In a large mixing bowl, mix together eggs, buttermilk, salt, pepper and tarragon.

Place mushrooms and onions in the bottom of partially baked pie crust. Spread with cheese. Pour egg mixture over top.

Place quiche in oven. Immediately reduce oven temperature to 350°. Bake about 35 minutes until set in center.

1 BUTTERMILK PIE CRUST (Add herbs to the dough, if desired)

1/4 cup chopped onion

8 ounces sliced mushrooms

2 tablespoons butter

4 eggs

1-1/3 cups buttermilk

1-1/2 teaspoons salt

1/2 teaspoon pepper

3/4 teaspoon dried tarragon

1-1/4 cups grated swiss or gruyere cheese

Preheat oven to 425°

NEAT JOSEPHINES

8 to 10 Dinner Rolls

Filling:

1/2 pound lean
  ground beef

1 small, minced onion

1 clove minced garlic

1/3 cup catsup

1/2 teaspoon chili
  powder

1/4 teaspoon ground
  cumin

1/4 teaspoon dried red
  pepper flakes

1/8 teaspoon dried
  oregano

Rolls:

4-1/2 cups all-purpose
  or bread flour

1 cup cornmeal

3 tablespoons sugar

1 teaspoon salt

1-1/2 cups buttermilk

1/4 cup butter

2 eggs

1 packet active dry
  yeast

cornmeal for dusting

Preheat oven to 375°

These mildly spiced "Sloppy Joes" tucked in a cornmeal roll make a great lunch box stuffer or a light supper.

Prepare filling: Brown meat, onion and garlic in a small skillet, breaking up meat finely with a fork. Drain off any fat. Add catsup, chili powder, cumin, pepper flakes and oregano. Cover skillet and simmer mixture 10 minutes. This filling may be made ahead and refrigerated up to 3 days. You may also adjust the "heat" by increasing or decreasing the amount of pepper flakes.

Prepare rolls: Mix flour, cornmeal, sugar and salt. Heat buttermilk and butter in a small saucepan until butter is just melted. This mixture may curdle.

Pour buttermilk mixture in large bowl and cool to lukewarm. Stir in eggs and yeast. Let proof about 10 minutes. Add flour mixture. Mix. Knead 8 to 10 minutes until smooth and elastic.

Turn dough in greased bowl. Cover and let rise about 1 hour until doubled. Cut dough in half. Divide each half into 4 or 5 equal portions and shape into balls.

Grease a baking sheet and dust with cornmeal.

Press and stretch each ball of dough to a 4" to 5" circle. Place a heaping teaspoon of filling in center. Tuck edges around and under to form round roll. Place seam down on prepared baking sheet. Cover and let rise until doubled, about 45 minutes.

Bake 20 minutes until golden brown. Serve hot. Store leftovers in refrigerator. Leftovers are best if reheated.

SAUERKRAUT GOULASH

Perfect fare for a hearth-side supper. Traditionally served over egg noodles, its lusty juices are just as well suited to a hunk of peasant bread.

In a heavy Dutch oven, heat oil. In batches, brown the meat on all sides, taking care that pieces do not touch. Set meat aside.

Sauté onions in drippings until softened. Add garlic and cook 1 minute longer.

Return the meat and any exuded juices to pan. Add salt, pepper and paprika and cook 1 minute. Add puree, water, sugar and bay leaf. Stir. Cover and simmer on low heat for 2 hours.

Stir in sauerkraut. Cover and simmer 45 minutes until meat is very tender.

Stir in buttermilk. Cook uncovered for 15 minutes. This dish is best if refrigerated overnight. Freezes well. Serve hot.

> Use deli or plastic-pouched sauerkraut from the grocer's cooler — not canned sauerkraut.

1/4 cup olive oil
2-1/2 pounds chuck roast, trimmed, cut in 1" cubes
2 large onions, sliced
1 clove crushed garlic
1 teaspoon salt
1/2 teaspoon freshly ground pepper
2 teaspoons sweet Hungarian paprika
15- or 16-ounce can tomato puree
1 cup water
1-1/2 tablespoons sugar
1 bay leaf
3 cups drained sauerkraut
1/2 cup buttermilk

SOOZANNA'S FRIED CHICKEN

4 to 6 Servings

2 cups buttermilk

4 to 6 dashes Tabasco sauce

3 to 4 pounds chicken pieces

1 cup all purpose flour

1 teaspoon salt

1/2 teaspoon freshly ground pepper

canola or other vegetable oil

Preheat oil to 375°

So-o-o simple. So-o-o delicious, hot or cold.

Mix buttermilk and Tabasco sauce in a sealable plastic bag or bowl. Add chicken. Turn to coat. Marinate in refrigerator at least 30 minutes, up to several hours.

Mix flour, salt and pepper in another bag. Remove chicken from marinade, allowing excess buttermilk to drip off. Shake chicken in flour one piece at a time.

Place on baking sheet and let sit about 15 minutes. Meanwhile, heat 4" to 5" of oil in a wok, very deep skillet or deep fryer. It's important to have the oil hot enough. Fry chicken a few pieces at a time until deep golden brown, about 15 to 20 minutes, turning as needed. Do not crowd.

Drain and serve or refrigerate.

TAJ MAHAL CHICKEN

The traditional Indian spices used in the batter for this chicken are a mild introduction to the wonderful flavors of Indian cuisine. Marinate the chicken overnight in the refrigerator to intensify the flavors.

In a sealable plastic bag, combine onion, garlic, ginger, coriander, cumin, salt, cloves, cinnamon, and cardamom.

Add lemon juice and buttermilk. Mix well.

With a sharp knife, slash each piece of chicken in several places to the bone.

Add chicken to buttermilk mixture. Massage to coat with the marinade. Chill several hours or overnight.

Bake 45 to 50 minutes until browned. May also be grilled.

1-1/2 cups chopped onion

3 cloves garlic, minced

1" slice fresh ginger, minced

1 teaspoon ground coriander

1 teaspoon ground cumin

1 teaspoon salt

1/4 teaspoon ground cloves

1/4 teaspoon cinnamon

1/4 teaspoon ground cardamom

2 tablespoons lemon juice

1/2 cup buttermilk

3 pounds chicken pieces

Preheat oven to 375°

Soups, Salads & Sides

SOUPS

As a light repast or a whole meal, soups range from simple and frugal peasant fare to elegant, intricately flavored potages. Buttermilk is a great finisher for many soups. It can replace higher-fat creams while lending both a slight tang and smooth texture.

It is true that a good stock, everything else being equal, will assure a better soup. We prefer to use homemade stock which we make in big batches and store in the freezer. Some canned stocks are adequate, but choose a variety that doesn't taste too salty. Toss those chemical cubes and salty soup base mixes away.

QUICK HOMEMADE CHICKEN STOCK

2 to 3 Quarts

Remove the excess fat from a four- to five-pound fowl or roasting hen, or use equal weight portions of chicken wings or backs. Place poultry in a large kettle. Add water to cover by one inch. Toss in two whole, peeled carrots and a whole large, unpeeled onion with its roots cut off. If desired, add small amounts of whole peppercorns, fresh parsley or other seasonings, but no salt.

Bring to a boil over medium-high heat, skimming off any protein scum that comes to the top. Cover partially. Reduce heat to a bare simmer and cook about 1-1/2 hours. Strain soup to remove solids. Chill until fats congeal on the top and then remove the fat, or try this tip: Line a colander with two layers of paper towels moistened with cold water. Pour the warm stock through the colander. The fats will stick to the paper towels.

QUICK HOMEMADE DARK BEEF STOCK

2 to 3 Quarts

Place four to five pounds of meaty beef soup bones in a roasting pan with one large peeled, halved onion and one or two peeled parsnips and carrots. Roast at 400° about 45 minutes until the bones have browned. Drain off fat. Place ingredients in a large kettle. Pour about one cup of water into the roasting pan and deglaze, scraping the bottom to loosen browned bits. Pour into kettle. Add more water to cover by one inch. If desired, add small amounts of whole peppercorns, fresh parsley or other seasonings, but no salt.

Bring to a boil over medium-high flame, skimming off any protein scum that comes to the top. Cover partially. Reduce heat to a bare simmer and cook about 1-1/2 hours. Strain soup to remove solids. Chill until fats congeal on the top and then remove the fat or try the paper towel-lined colander trick described above.

BACON and CARROT SPLIT PEA SOUP

6 Servings

If you're like us, you occasionally have a craving for split pea soup but hesitate to make the usual umpteen-gallon recipes. Here's a small batch that is easily doubled.

In a heavy saucepan, sauté bacon until almost crisp. Add onions and carrot. Sauté 10 minutes until onion is soft. Add peas, salt, pepper, savory and stock. Simmer uncovered 1 hour, stirring occasionally, until peas are soft. Stir in buttermilk and serve.

> For an even heartier soup, add one or two peeled, diced potatoes with the peas.

- 5 slices of bacon cut in 1/2" pieces
- 1 cup minced onion
- 1 cup diced carrot
- 1 cup dried, split green peas
- 1 teaspoon salt
- 1/2 teaspoon freshly ground pepper
- 1/2 teaspoon dried summer savory
- 4 cups of favorite stock or water
- 1/2 cup buttermilk

CREAM OF BROCCOLI and LEEK SOUP

6 to 8 Servings

Frugal cooks can substitute vitamin-rich broccoli stems saved from another recipe. Just peel off the tough outer layer of the larger stalks.

In a medium-size, heavy saucepan melt butter. Sauté leeks until tender.

Meanwhile, grate potato into 1 cup of water.

Add broth, undrained potato, broccoli, salt, pepper and cayenne to leeks. Bring to a boil. Reduce heat and simmer until broccoli is tender, about 15 minutes. Remove from heat and let cool slightly.

Puree soup in blender or food processor.

Return to pan and whisk in buttermilk. Adjust seasoning. Heat to serving temperature. Do not boil.

- 2 tablespoons butter
- 3 leeks, coarsely chopped
- 4 cups chicken broth
- 1 cup water
- 1 small potato, peeled
- florets of 1 large bunch of broccoli, cut into 1/2" pieces
- 1/2 teaspoon salt
- 1/4 teaspoon freshly ground black pepper
- 1/4 teaspoon cayenne pepper
- 1 cup buttermilk

DREAMING of the CARIBBEAN CARROT SOUP

6 Servings

1 tablespoon butter

1 cup chopped onion

2 cups sliced carrots

1-1/2 teaspoons peeled, grated gingerroot

1 cup water

2 cups chicken stock

2 teaspoons grated orange zest

1/2 teaspoon honey

1/2 teaspoon salt

1/4 teaspoon freshly ground pepper

1/4 teaspoon ground cumin

1/4 teaspoon ground cardamom

1 tablespoon rum (optional)

1/2 cup buttermilk

Like the fine, warm particles of sand on a beach, the combination of many small amounts of seasonings in this soup results in a smooth, sensuous experience.

Over medium heat, in a medium size saucepan, melt butter. Add onion and sauté until just tender. Add carrots and gingerroot. Cover and cook 5 minutes. Add water and stock and bring to a boil.

Reduce heat to medium-low. Cover and cook until carrots are tender. Remove 1/2 cup of solid vegetables from the soup and set aside. Puree remaining soup until smooth.

Return solids and pureed soup to the pan. Stir in seasonings, rum and buttermilk.

> A garnish of chopped cilantro or parsley is nice.

SQUASH SOUP with an AFRICAN BEAT

6 Servings

An astonishingly delicious but simple to make soup.

In a medium-size saucepan, sauté onions in oil until soft. Add garlic and ginger and sauté 1 minute. Stir in peanut butter. Add squash, stock, cayenne, coriander, salt and Worcestershire sauce. Simmer 15 minutes on low heat until thickened. Add buttermilk. Heat to serving temperature, taking care not to boil.

> For a fancier presentation, garnish servings with chopped scallion greens and chopped roasted peanuts.

1-1/2 teaspoons vegetable oil

1 cup finely chopped onion

2 cloves minced garlic

2" minced fresh gingerroot

4 tablespoons extra-crunchy peanut butter

2 cups cooked or 12 ounces frozen, thawed, mashed winter squash

2 cups chicken stock

pinch cayenne pepper or more to taste

1/4 teaspoon ground coriander

1/2 teaspoon salt

1 teaspoon Worcestershire or Pickapeppa sauce

3/4 cup buttermilk, or more for desired consistency

TWO BEAN BISQUE

12 Servings

1 cup dried Great Northern beans

1 cup dried chick peas

1 tablespoon olive oil

2 cups chopped onion

2 cloves garlic, minced

1 ham bone with meat or a 5-ounce piece of ham

4 cups chicken broth

1 small, peeled, chopped turnip

2 carrots, coarsely chopped

dash cayenne pepper

1/2 teaspoon freshly ground black pepper

1/4 teaspoon dried dill

3/4 cup buttermilk

A hearty, healthy potage.

In separate bowls, cover the beans with cold water. Soak overnight or quick soak. (Bring beans to a boil. Boil for 2 minutes. Remove from heat and cover. Let stand for 1 hour.) Drain beans.

In a large soup kettle, sauté the onions in the oil until tender. Add garlic and sauté 1 minute. Add the drained Great Northern beans, ham bone, broth and turnip. Simmer about 1-1/2 hours until beans are very tender. Remove ham and set aside.

Meanwhile, cook the chick peas in water to cover about 45 minutes until almost tender. Add the carrots and cook about 25 minutes until carrots are tender. Drain.

Once the Great Northern beans are very tender, remove soup from heat and mash well. Add cayenne, black pepper and dill. Stir in drained chick peas and carrots. Chop and return ham, if desired.

Stir in buttermilk. Adjust seasoning. Reheat if necessary but do not boil. Serve hot.

WINTER COMFORT POTATO SOUP

A very plain, filling peasant soup that is quick and simple to make. Perfect as is for a quick lunch, or toss in some leftover vegetables and serve with bread and butter for a simple supper.

Melt butter in medium saucepan over low heat. Add onion. Sauté about 5 minutes until onions are soft but not browned.

Add potatoes cut in 1" to 2" chunks. Add water. Potatoes should be just covered. Bring to a boil. Reduce heat to medium-high and simmer 20 minutes until potatoes are very soft. Remove from heat.

Mash with potato masher to make a coarse puree. Add buttermilk and seasonings. Reheat gently if necessary. Serve hot, garnished with additional butter, grated sharp cheddar cheese or chives for a special touch.

1 tablespoon butter
1 cup diced onion
3 medium peeled, boiling potatoes
2 cups water
1/2 cup buttermilk
1 teaspoon salt
freshly ground pepper to taste

BACON POTATO SALAD

4 Servings

Dressing:

2 tablespoons
  mayonnaise

1 tablespoon red wine
  vinegar

2 teaspoons sugar

1/2 teaspoon salt

1/4 teaspoon coarsely
  ground black pepper

1/4 cup buttermilk

Salad:

2 pounds boiling
  potatoes (4 to 5
  medium)

1/3 cup finely chopped
  red onion

1 stalk celery, thinly
  sliced

4 slices crisp, cooked
  bacon, chopped

1/2 teaspoon celery
  seed (optional)

*This simple potato salad is good served hot,
warm or cold.*

Dressing:

Whisk together mayonnaise, vinegar, sugar,
salt and pepper until smooth. Stir in
buttermilk.

Salad:

Boil potatoes until tender. Drain. Peel if
desired.

Cut into chunks.

In a large bowl, toss hot potatoes with
dressing to coat well. Stir in onions, celery,
bacon and celery seed.

Refrigerate leftovers.

BUTTERMILK POTATO SALAD

8 to 10 Servings

An American-style potato salad. Make this a day ahead to meld the flavors.

Place potatoes and eggs in large pot with cold water to cover. Bring to boil. Remove eggs after 15 minutes and chill in cold water. Continue cooking potatoes for 10 minutes until very tender.

Meanwhile, mix buttermilk, mustard, vinegar, oil, sugar, salt and pepper. Stir in onion and celery. Peel, dice and add eggs.

Drain potatoes. Peel if desired. Cut in 1/2" dice. Add hot potatoes to dressing mixture, stirring to coat. Cover and chill overnight.

Serve chilled.

This recipe may be halved.

4 pounds unpeeled boiling potatoes

4 eggs

1/2 cup buttermilk

2 tablespoons dijon-style mustard

4 tablespoons cider vinegar

2 tablespoons olive oil

1 tablespoon sugar

1 teaspoon salt

1/2 teaspoon coarsely ground black pepper

1/2 cup minced red onion

3 stalks sliced celery

BARLEY BUTTERMILK SUMMER SALAD

12 Servings

1-1/2 cups pearl
barley

8 cups cold water

2 teaspoons salt

1/2 cup mayonnaise

1 cup buttermilk

3/4 cup freshly grated
parmesan cheese

2 tablespoons red
wine vinegar

1 teaspoon coarsely
ground black pepper

2 cups fresh or frozen
corn kernels

1 cup fresh or frozen
peas

7-ounce jar roasted
red peppers, drained
and chopped in 1/2"
pieces

4 scallions, whites and
tender green tops,
thinly sliced

Once you introduce this salad at picnics, your friends will ask for it again and again. Bring copies of the recipe!

Place barley in a strainer and rinse well under cold water. Place barley in medium-size, heavy saucepan with water and salt. Bring to a boil. Reduce heat to medium-low and partially cover. Simmer until just tender, stirring occasionally, about 25 minutes. Drain.

In a medium-size bowl, whisk mayonnaise with buttermilk, cheese, vinegar and pepper until smooth.

Mix barley, corn, peas, peppers and scallions. Gently toss with dressing.

Serve chilled.

This salad keeps well in the refrigerator.

BROCCOLI & BEEF SALAD
with BLUE CHEESE DRESSING

Serves 10 to 12

This salad is a striking addition to any buffet table.

Remove stalks from broccoli, reserving for other uses. Trim florets to about 1" pieces. Blanch florets in boiling water about 5 minutes. Drain under cold running water to stop cooking. Let drain and set aside.

Mix buttermilk with sugar, salt and pepper. Stir in cheese, onion, vinegar, parsley and garlic. Fold in beef and broccoli florets. Chill 1 hour or longer to meld flavors.

To serve, place greens on large platter. Spoon beef mixture on top. Garnish with parsley.

1 bunch broccoli

1 cup buttermilk

1 teaspoon sugar

1/4 teaspoon salt

1/4 teaspoon freshly ground pepper

4 ounces blue cheese, crumbled

1/2 cup minced red onion

4 tablespoons red wine or cider vinegar

6 tablespoons minced fresh parsley

4 cloves roasted garlic or 1 clove fresh garlic, crushed

2 cups cooked rare roast beef, cut in 1/2" cubes

about 4 cups assorted mixed salad greens

chopped parsley for garnish

CURRIED PORK and RICE SALAD
with DRIED CHERRIES

8 to 10 Servings

Salad:

1-1/2 cups raw rice, preferably basmati or other aromatic rice

3 cups water

2 to 3 cups cooked pork, cut in 1/2" cubes

1/2 cup thinly sliced celery

1/2 cup minced scallion or red onion

Dressing:

1/2 cup mayonnaise

1/2 cup buttermilk

1 tablespoon lemon juice or red wine vinegar

1-1/2 teaspoons sugar

1 teaspoon salt

1-1/2 teaspoons good quality curry powder

1/2 cup dried cherries, raisins or dried cranberries

1 cup unsalted roasted cashews for garnish

An absolutely delicious way to use leftover pork roast or chops. The dried cherries add interesting taste and color. Good either warm or cold.

Salad:

In a medium-size saucepan, over medium heat, bring rice and water to boil. Cover and reduce heat to low. Cook about 15 minutes until rice is done. Place rice in a large bowl. Set aside to cool.

Add pork, celery and onions to cooled rice.

Dressing:

In a medium-size bowl, whisk together mayonnaise and buttermilk until smooth. Stir in lemon juice, sugar, salt, curry powder and dried cherries.

Toss salad with dressing. Garnish with cashews just before serving.

GOOD FOR YOU BUTTERMILK TABOULEH

4 to 6 Servings

Here's a healthy, hearty lunch or side dish salad.

Salad:

Soak bulgur in 4 cups hot tap water for 30 minutes. Transfer to colander. Drain for at least 10 minutes. Squeeze dry by handfuls and place in a bowl.

In a food processor, chop parsley and scallions until fine. Add to bulgur with chick peas, cucumber and tomatoes.

Dressing:

In processor, whip together buttermilk, olive oil, mint, garlic, lemon juice, salt and pepper.

Stir dressing into salad. Chill well before serving.

Salad:
1-1/2 cups bulgur
1 bunch parsley
4 large minced scallions
1 cup cooked chick peas
1 peeled, seeded, minced cucumber
2 diced tomatoes

Dressing:
1 cup buttermilk
1/4 cup extra-virgin olive oil
1 scant tablespoon dried mint leaves
1 clove garlic, minced
2 tablespoons lemon juice or wine vinegar
1 teaspoon salt
1 tablespoon coarsely ground black pepper

GREEK LENTIL SALAD

8 to 10 Servings

Salad:

1 cup lentils

3 cups water

4 pepperoncini (mild pickled peppers), stemmed, seeded and chopped

3/4 cup halved black olives

1/2 chopped red onion

4 ounces feta cheese, cubed

1 medium cucumber, peeled, seeded and chopped

Dressing:

1/4 cup mayonnaise

1/2 cup buttermilk

1 teaspoon oregano

2 tablespoons red wine vinegar

2 teaspoons sugar

1/4 teaspoon coarsely ground black pepper

This is a very satisfying salad with a wonderful variety of textures and tastes. It's also a perfect pita bread stuffing.

Salad:

In a medium-size saucepan, bring lentils and water to a boil. Reduce heat and simmer 15 minutes until firm, but tender. Drain. Cool slightly. Add pepperoncini, olives, onion, feta and cucumber.

Dressing:

Whisk together mayonnaise and buttermilk. Stir in oregano, vinegar, sugar and pepper. Mix well.

Toss salad with dressing. Chill well before serving.

KASHA WALDORF SALAD

This recipe is loosely based on two classic recipes — Kasha Varnishkas and Waldorf Salad. It is a delightful way to introduce your family to vitamin-packed kasha.

Dressing:

Whisk together mayonnaise, buttermilk, orange juice, sugar and salt. Set aside.

Salad:

In a small bowl, beat egg. Add kasha and toss with egg to completely coat. Set aside.

In a small saucepan, bring water, salt, pepper and butter to a boil.

Meanwhile, heat a large skillet over medium-high heat. Add kasha to the dry skillet and stir constantly 1-1/2 to 2 minutes until the grains are separated and toasted, taking care not to burn. Add the boiling water mixture. Reduce heat to very low. Stir briefly and cover tightly. Cook 8 minutes or longer until grains are tender.

Combine pasta and kasha with the dressing. Stir in walnuts, raisins, apples and celery.

Serve cold or at room temperature.

> Kasha is roasted buckwheat kernels. Find it in the ethnic section of your supermarket. We used medium grind in this recipe.

Dressing:
1 tablespoon mayonnaise
2 tablespoons buttermilk
2 tablespoons freshly squeezed orange juice
1 teaspoon sugar
pinch of salt

Salad:
1 egg
1/2 cup kasha
1 cup water
1/4 teaspoon salt
pinch of freshly ground pepper
1 tablespoon butter
1 cup uncooked farfelle (bowtie pasta), cooked according to package directions
1/2 cup coarsely chopped, toasted walnuts
1/2 cup raisins
1 small, unpeeled chopped Granny Smith (green) apple
1 small, unpeeled chopped Empire (red) apple
1 stalk celery, thinly sliced

RAINBOW COLE SLAW

6 to 8 Servings

1-1/2 cups buttermilk

1/2 cup slivered or grated red onion

4 tablespoons cider vinegar

1 tablespoon sugar

1 teaspoon salt

1 teaspoon freshly ground pepper

1 cup julienned or grated carrot

1/4 cup julienned or minced celery

1 small green cabbage, julienned or minced

1/2 small red cabbage, julienned or minced

If you prefer a sweeter slaw, mince the vegetables into smaller pieces. Make this salad a day ahead to allow the flavors to meld. The red cabbage will dye the dressing pink. Drain before serving.

Mix buttermilk, onion, vinegar, sugar, salt and pepper until sugar is dissolved.

Add carrot, celery and cabbages. Cover and refrigerate overnight, stirring frequently to distribute the dressing.

This recipe is easily halved.

BACON BUTTERMILK SALAD DRESSING

About 1 Cup

1/2 cup mayonnaise

1/2 cup buttermilk

2 chopped scallions

2 tablespoons chopped parsley

1 clove minced garlic

1/2 teaspoon freshly ground pepper

1/4 teaspoon salt

dash Tabasco sauce

6 slices bacon, cooked crisp, crumbled

Whisk mayonnaise and buttermilk until smooth. Stir in scallions, parsley, garlic, pepper, salt and Tabasco sauce. Stir in bacon. Chill at least 1 hour to blend flavors.

> For BACON HORSERADISH SALAD DRESSING, add 2 to 3 teaspoons drained prepared horse-radish.

WINE and CHEESE PEPPERCORN SALAD DRESSING

About 3 Cups

Puree buttermilk, wine, vinegar, parmesan, garlic and salt in food processor until well mixed. With motor running, add olive oil in a thin stream, processing until emulsified. Stir in pepper. Store dressing in refrigerator. Process or whisk again before serving if oil separates.

1 cup buttermilk

1/2 cup good dry white wine

1/4 cup cider vinegar

1/2 cup shaved parmesan cheese

1 clove garlic, minced or mashed

1 teaspoon salt

1 cup olive oil

1 teaspoon coarsely ground black pepper

GORGONZOLA SALAD DRESSING

About 1-3/4 Cups

The marriage of buttermilk and blue cheese makes one of the most classic salad dressings.

Whisk mayonnaise, vinegar and buttermilk until smooth. Stir in cheese, salt and pepper. Chill at least 1 hour to blend flavors.

1/2 cup mayonnaise

1 tablespoon balsamic vinegar

3/4 cup buttermilk

1/4 pound mashed gorgonzola or crumbled blue cheese

1/4 teaspoon salt

1/2 teaspoon freshly ground pepper

GARLIC LEMON SALAD DRESSING

About 1-1/4 Cups

1 cup buttermilk

1 large crushed garlic clove

1/4 cup sour cream

1/4 teaspoon dry mustard

2 teaspoons fresh lemon juice

1/2 teaspoon coarsely cracked pepper

This dressing is good on green salads. With a little onion, it makes great tuna fish salad.

Mix all ingredients well in blender or food processor until smooth. Chill at least 2 hours to blend flavors.

BUTTERMILK RANCH SALAD DRESSING

1-1/2 Cups

1 cup buttermilk

1/2 cup mayonnaise

1 teaspoon white wine vinegar

1 tablespoon minced fresh parsley

2 cloves minced garlic

3/4 teaspoon onion powder

1/2 teaspoon dried marjoram

1/4 teaspoon celery seed

1/4 teaspoon freshly ground black pepper

1/4 teaspoon salt

A perennial favorite!

Whisk buttermilk, mayonnaise and vinegar until smooth. Stir in remaining ingredients. Chill 2 hours to blend flavors.

BUTTERMILK MASHED POTATOES

6 Servings

Buttermilk makes the most delicious mashed potatoes. Besides the advantage of being lower in fat than milk or cream, buttermilk adds a subtle new taste to this old standby.

Peel potatoes. Cut in quarters. Cover with cold water and boil until tender, 15 to 20 minutes. Drain well. Return the pot to the burner briefly, shaking to drive off excess moisture. Mash. Add butter, salt and pepper. Add buttermilk, adding more if needed for desired consistency.

Variations: Stir 1/4 cup chopped, fresh chives, minced scallion, 3 or more cloves of mashed ROASTED GARLIC, or 1/4 cup parmesan cheese into the mashed potatoes.

4 medium-large
  potatoes
2 tablespoons butter
salt and pepper to
  taste
6 tablespoons
  buttermilk

ROASTED GARLIC

The new staple of the '90s, freshly roasted garlic has a mild, almost nutty flavor. Try it spread on crackers or warm bread.

Frozen heads of roasted garlic ensure a ready supply for your favorite recipes.

Remove any loose skin from a full head of garlic. Slice about 1/2" off the top of the head to reveal the individual cloves. Sprinkle the head with olive oil. Wrap in aluminum foil and bake at 350° for 35 to 40 minutes, until garlic is very soft.

To use, just pop the garlic cloves out of their skin.

CORNBREAD and BISCUIT DRESSING

10 Servings

4 tablespoons butter, divided

2 large onions, chopped

1/2 cup chopped celery

3 cups crumbled cornbread

3 cups crumbled biscuits

1/2 teaspoon thyme

salt and pepper to taste

2 teaspoons poultry seasoning

1 tablespoon chopped fresh sage or 1-1/2 teaspoons dried

4 beaten eggs

3 cups chicken stock

Preheat oven to 375°

Testing recipes often yields interesting results. The idea for this wonderful stuffing came about when we were trying to make room in the freezer.

Melt 2 tablespoons butter in a 9" x 13" pan in preheating oven, taking care not to burn.

Melt 2 tablespoons butter in a large skillet. Add onion and celery and cook until tender but not browned. Mix cornbread and biscuit crumbs in large bowl. Add thyme, salt, pepper, poultry seasoning and sage. Stir in eggs and as much stock as needed to reach desired consistency.

Pour into prepared pan. Bake 45 minutes or longer until top is browned.

This mixture can also be prepared as FRIED STUFFING CAKES.

Add stock as needed until mixture can be formed into small cakes. Fry in skillet in butter, meat drippings or oil over medium low heat. Turn gently to brown on both sides.

RAISIN CORNBREAD DRESSING

About 2 Quarts

Use day-old, or older, cornbread to make this stunning side dish for roasted chicken or turkey breast.

Crumble cornbread finely into large bowl. Set aside.

Cook bacon until crisp. Remove bacon and drain, reserving drippings.

Crumble bacon and add to cornbread with raisins, mixing well. Sprinkle with 3 tablespoons bacon drippings, tossing to distribute.

Drizzle mixture with stock, using as much as required to lightly moisten all of the crumbs.

Turn mixture into greased 2 quart casserole.

Bake about 30 minutes until golden on top.

This stuffing can be baked at lower or higher temperatures to match other dishes in the oven. Serve hot. Store leftovers in refrigerator. Reheat before serving.

1/2 recipe
SOUTHERN
MAMA'S MOIST
CORNBREAD
8 to 10 slices bacon
1-1/2 cups raisins
2 cups chicken stock

Preheat oven to 350°

CORN OYSTERS

About 8 Fritters

1/2 cup all-purpose
flour
1 teaspoon sugar
1/2 teaspoon baking
soda
1/2 teaspoon salt
1 egg, beaten
1/3 cup buttermilk
1-1/4 cups thawed
frozen or cooked
corn
1 cup vegetable oil
real maple syrup

*The closest thing to a healthy doughnut.
They're also good as a side dish. For fruit
fritters, increase the sugar and substitute
fruits or berries for the corn.*

In a large mixing bowl, combine flour, sugar,
baking soda and salt.

In a separate bowl, combine egg and
buttermilk.

Combine egg mixture and dry ingredients.
Stir in corn.

In a heavy skillet, heat oil over medium-low
heat. Drop mixture by heaping tablespoons
into oil. Cook about 3 minutes per side until
browned.

Serve immediately with maple syrup.

RUSSIAN-STYLE BAKED MUSHROOMS

4 Servings

Serve these tasty mushrooms as a side dish with grilled meats.

In a large skillet over medium heat, melt butter. Sauté onions until softened. Add mushrooms. Cook until mushrooms have darkened and most of the exuded juices have evaporated.

Stir in flour until completely absorbed. Cook, stirring continuously, 2 minutes. Add salt, pepper and buttermilk. Stir briefly until sauce is slightly thickened. Do not boil.

Turn into a small, buttered casserole dish. Sprinkle with cheese and paprika.

Bake 15 minutes until cheese is melted. Serve hot.

3 tablespoons butter

1/2 cup finely chopped onion

12 ounces thickly sliced mushrooms

2-1/2 tablespoons all-purpose flour

salt and pepper to taste

1 cup buttermilk

2 tablespoons grated cheese (parmesan, romano or cheddar)

paprika for sprinkling

Preheat oven to 350°

BUTTERMILK QUANTITY INDEX

If you're wondering what to make with what's left in the carton, here's a handy index by the amount of buttermilk required for all the recipes in this book. Page numbers are in the regular index.

4 cups

Homemade Cheese ....
Sparkling Orange Punch ....
Spicy Peach Cooler ....

2 cups

Bacon Muenster Soda Bread ....
Baked Maple Pecan Chicken ....
Basic White Bread ....
Cajun Fried Chicken ....
Caraway Cheese Coins ....
Cinnamon Rolls ....
Easy Corn Waffles ....
Lemon Buttermilk Chiffon Sherbet ....
Maple-Kissed Buttermilk Bread ....
Marzipan Swirl Loaf ....
Maui Sherbet ....
Modern Macaroni and Cheese ....
Multi-Grain Pancakes ....
Soozanna's Fried Chicken ....
Southern Mama's Moist Cornbread ....
Sticky Buns ....
Sweet Bread Dough ....
Sweet Cheese Rolls ....

1-1/2 cups

Anna's Apple Coffee Cake ....
Dairy Challah ....
Everyday Chocolate Cake ....
Neat Josephines ....
Rainbow Cole Slaw ....

1-1/3 cups

Mushroom Quiche ....

1-1/4 cups

Buttermilk Waffles ....
Sun-Dried Tomato Bread ....
Toasted Coconut Layer Cake ....

1 cup

Adult Raisin Pancakes ....
Angel Wing Yeast Biscuits ....
Bacon Dumplings ....
Banana Pecan Muffins ....
Banana Walnut Pancakes ....
Barley Buttermilk Summer Salad ....
Basic Buttermilk Pancakes ....
Basic Muffin Batter ....
Best Restaurant Biscuits ....
Blueberry Cornmeal Pancakes ....
Blueberry Muffins ....
Blueberry Pancakes ....
Broccoli and Beef Salad with Blue Cheese
    Dressing ....
Buttermilk Bagels ....
Buttermilk Bread Pudding with Butter-
    scotch Sauce ....
Buttermilk Cake Doughnuts ....
Buttermilk Dumplings ....
Buttermilk Meatloaf ....
Buttermilk Raisin Pie ....
Buttermilk Ranch Salad Dressing ....
Cape Cod Smoothie ....
Caramel Frosting ....
Cheddar Popovers ....
Cherry Muffins ....
Chili and Cornbread Casserole ....
Chocolate Toasted Almond Ice Cream .....
Cornmeal Dumplings ....
Cranberry Lime Cake ....
Cream of Broccoli and Leek Soup ....
Family Raisin Pancakes ....
Fig or Date Muffins ....
Frozen Pumpkin Patch, The (frozen
    dessert) ....
Garlic Lemon Salad Dressing ....
Good for You Buttermilk Tabouleh ....
Green and Gold Rice Casserole ....
Herb Dumplings ....
Honey Buckwheat Currant Brown
    Bread ....
Jelly Cupboard Cake ....
Jelly Doughnut Muffins ....
Lemon Curd Coffee Cake with Lemon
    Glaze ....

BUTTERMILK QUANTITY INDEX

Buttermilk Potato Salad ....
Buttermilk Almond Rum Balls ....
Butterscotch Sauce ....
Caramelized Onion, Wild Mushroom and
  Stilton Pizza ....
Cheese Pizza Crust ....
Chinese Pizza ....
Chocolate Frosted Smooches
  (cookies) ....
Chocolate Mocha Cheesecake ....
Chocolate Waffles, Please... ....
Classic Chocolate Chip Cookies ....
Cobbler Dough ....
Coca-Cola Cake with Coca-Cola Icing .....
Coconut Pie ....
Cornmeal or Semolina Pizza Crust ....
Cranberry Hazelnut Oatmeal Cookies ......
Curried Pork and Rice Salad with Dried
  Cherries ....
Dilled Feta Cheese Bread ....
Double Cherry Cobbler ....
Dreaming of the Caribbean Carrot
  Soup ....
Drop Biscuit Shortcakes ....
Faux-caccia ....
Garlic and Herb Pizza Crust ....
Ginger Pear Shortcake with Ginger
  Custard Sauce ....
Gorgonzola Salad Dressing ....
Greek Lentil Salad ....
Greek Pizza ....
Harvest Spice Cake ....
Honolulu Pizza ....
Kielbasa Sauerkraut Rye Loaf ....
New Delhi Curry Dip ....
Not Kosher Chopped Chicken Liver ....
Peach Molasses Upside Down Cake ....
Pesto Pizza ....
Plain Ol' Sugar Cookies ....
Praline Peach Cobbler ....
Pumpkin Pecan Cheesecake ....
Rolled Biscuit Shortcakes ....
Roquefort, Walnut and Red Onion
  Pizza ....
Rum Runners Molasses Drops ....
Sauerkraut Goulash ....
Soft Hermit Bars ....
South of the Border Pizza ....
Spinach Ricotta Pizza with Roasted Red
  Peppers ....
Springtime in Siberia Radish Dip ....
Sugar Plum Coffee Cake ....

Taj Mahal Chicken ....
White Garlic Pizza ....
Whole Wheat Oatmeal Bread ....
Whole Wheat Pizza Crust ....
Winter Comfort Potato Soup ....

1/3 cup

Black Forest Jumbles ....
Buttermilk Mashed Potatoes ....
Buttermilk Pie Crust ....
Corn Oysters ....
New Age Pimento Cheese Spread ....

1/4 cup

Bacon Potato Salad ....
Cajun Shrimp Dip ....
Giant Tropical Jewels ....
Glazed Bing Cherry Coffee Cake ....
Mango Mambo Sherbet ....
Marion's Fruit Cake Winks ....
Pumpkin Walnut Scones ....
S'More Brownies ....
Semi-Sweet Florentines ....

Less than 1/4 cup

Crème Fraîche ....
Spiced Honey Plums ....
Creamy Chocolate Frosting ....
Kasha Waldorf Salad ....

Buttermilk Cookbook: The Rest of the Carton

Buttermilk Cookbook: The Rest of the Carton

INDEX